T0283330

WEALTH
IS A
MINDSET

THIRD
STATE
BOOKS

SAN FRANCISCO

WEALTH
IS A
MINDSET

SHANG
SAAVEDRA

FOUNDER, SAVE MY CENTS

THIRD
STATE
BOOKS

THIRD STATE BOOKS

Third State Books
93 Cumberland Street
San Francisco, CA 94110
Visit us at www.thirdstatebooks.com

First edition: January 2025
Edited by Stephanie Lim with Charles Kim

ISBN 979-8-89013-026-6 (hardcover)
979-8-89013-027-3 (e-book)

Book design by Sandy Micone
Graphics by Hopp Creative
Printed in Canada by Transcontinental

To my parents for giving me the gift of financial literacy.

To my husband and in-laws for all your support and help.

To my children: I love you.

To everyone who has supported Save My Cents since I was just rambling on the internet: This book is for you.

Philippians 4:13

Thank you to Stephanie Lim and the team at Third State Books, who made this book possible and brought it to life. Thanks also to Sandy Micone for translating multiple ideas for the cover into one that was simple and powerful; and to Hopp Creative for being my graphics and branding team through the years. Lastly, thanks go to my early readers, who gave me crucial and honest feedback that helped shape the book into what it is today.

CONTENTS

YOUR MONEY STORY

Personal finance is personal. Your feelings and emotions about money are valid no matter how positive or negative they are, and there is no right or wrong way to feel about money.

Perhaps you have never learned about personal finance, and this is your first personal finance book. Welcome! It could be that it's January, and you set a new year's resolution to tackle your credit card debt. I'm so happy that you chose my book to help yourself. Maybe you shoulder a burdensome amount of student loans and don't see a path toward debt freedom. I'm glad you're here. Maybe you are like me, someone who grew up in a household that discussed money all the time, and you have strong and anxious feelings about money that don't seem to go away. I feel you. I wrote this book for anyone who wishes to take a deep look at their personal finances and make a change to improve their lives. It could be your first try at learning about personal finance, or maybe one of many attempts. This book is designed to be reread and increases in complexity, chapter by chapter, to meet you where you are. This book is also beneficial for beginning investors, especially those who have been at it for fewer than five years. If you are already retired or no longer need to work to cover your living expenses, this book is probably not for you.

When I talk about money, I know that I invite judgment. I've received all kinds of comments from strangers on social media when I write about personal finance: *Why do you buy clothes secondhand? Are you trying to look like you have no money? Why do you eat this kind of food? It looks so unappetizing. Why don't you spend money on your teeth if you claim to be so wealthy?* While personal finance uses numbers as its input, what truly matters are the intangible things that make you who you are: your money story. It is the story of your life and how it relates to money. It includes things such as how you grew up around money. Whether you learned anything formally regarding personal finance. How your closest family members, friends, and community behaved with money. When you got your first paycheck and what you did with it. All that information feeds into your money story.

Your money story is what matters when it comes to this book. Your history, your experiences, and what you are going through right now—these are the memories I want you to recall when reading this book. And as those vignettes and scenes float to the surface, I want you to open your mind to just one idea: Your money story can change for the better. I want you to live a more joyful life. I want you to find peace. I want you to achieve goals that you thought you could only dream of, and in the process of doing so, feel like you are the best version of yourself. That is the true power of financial freedom.

Let me share with you my money story.

My family came from humble beginnings in the People's Republic of China. My paternal grandfather was jailed during the Cultural Revolution on what my family believed were trumped-up charges, and my illiterate paternal grandmother had to figure out how to feed all her children and pay an exorbitant fine to free my grandfather. She hustled as an seamstress, and my father and his siblings made do with meager rations and homemade toys. My mother's family fared a bit better, but everyone had the same government rations of just one pound of pork a month per person.

My father was exceptionally bright. He tested first out of ten million students in his local province on the college exams, an extraordinary accomplishment that led to a full-ride scholarship to Tsinghua University, China's most prestigious engineering school. Afterward, he was granted permission to leave the country to pursue his graduate studies, first for a PhD in the Netherlands, then onward to working at a research center in Switzerland. We moved constantly to save money. Eventually, he found a job at the Massachusetts Institute of Technology in Cambridge, Massachusetts. As my father had the opportunity of a lifetime to leave behind a financially unstable past through education, he wanted me to go even further. Education was my be-all and end-all from a young age. My parents' approach to parenting mirrored that of many other Chinese American immigrants who saw education as the golden ticket to freedom and upward mobility. They adhered to a strict parenting style described as "Tiger parenting," a concept made famous by Amy Chua in her memoir, *Battle Hymn of the Tiger Mother.*

School and academics came quickly to me, whether it was history, geography, math, reading, or writing. Because my parents put so much emphasis on the value of education, getting into a top university was my only purpose in life. Nothing else mattered—and I was made to feel that *I* didn't matter if I didn't fulfill that singular goal. In my diary, I noted every time I didn't listen in class, stumbled over something in the homework, or felt that I should have done something better. I dreaded dinners because there would be a lecture whenever I came home with anything less than 100 on an exam. It would start with why I didn't get full marks, then end with the conclusion that people don't get into Ivy League schools by being careless and lazy.

I was very lonely. I never made my excitement for learning a secret, and that made me a target for bullying. There was bullying, both physical bullying—being tripped going downstairs or grabbed and poked against my will—and emotional. Classmates wrote disparagingly about me in other people's yearbooks. One very humiliating experience happened at church during dress rehearsal for a holiday concert. A boy in my Sunday school class pulled the piano bench from under me when I approached the stage in front of the entire children's choir. As he ran away cackling, the only person who came to comfort me was the choir conductor. Not only did I feel physical pain from landing on my tailbone, I felt emotional distress that my passionate personality made me unlikable to everyone else.

I had very few coping mechanisms for the pressure and pain I experienced. I directed my energy to accomplishments, hoping that would pay off somehow. My parents rarely praised me, though I didn't blame them. I never felt what

I achieved was enough. I needed to do more. I needed to do the most. So I won nearly every piano competition I entered, got mostly A's, and kept a high GPA—and I was extremely depressed throughout. As I reflected on my anxiety and tried to find solutions, I decided that getting rich would solve my problems. Perhaps I should aim to get into Harvard, become the CEO of a company, make a ton of money, and be written about in magazines. This way, I would make my parents proud, and they'd say "We love you" more often. And I would also be accepted by the world for not backing down from who I was. Ambition was the one power that I had in overabundant supply. This was to be my life's manifesto. I literally committed this to my diary during my high-school years.

I attended Harvard for my undergraduate studies. I pursued a degree in economics because I didn't want the long journey of medical school, and businesspeople seemed to do quite well. I landed a high-paying job in management consulting and also began a side hustle as a wedding photographer. I often worked up to ninety hours a week in those early years, quickly racking up over $100,000 in annual earnings across my two jobs. My parents taught me well about personal finance, which made them exceptional in this aspect of parenting. They emphasized frugality and hard work, showed me what a basic budget looked like, and told me to avoid credit card debt when I started to make money. In my final high-school years, my father also shared with me briefly the concept of investing. As a young adult, I tried to follow my parents' lead and save as much money as possible. Two girlfriends and I found a below-market Boston rental in a convenient downtown location, close to public transportation and my work so that I didn't have to buy a car. I ordered food through work whenever I could and ate leftovers for lunch the next day. After establishing a three-month emergency fund, I focused on putting my money into a 401(k) retirement account provided by my employer as well as a personal Roth Individual Retirement Arrangement. Any profits from my freelance photography work went into a taxable brokerage account. By the time I entered business school at age twenty-five, I had a six-figure net worth. My goal was simple: To become a CEO so that no one could ever call me weak or unaccomplished. And yet my mind was slowly crumbling from what my parents' voices were saying inside my head and also from my own sense of perfectionism and stubbornness to fulfill my high-school manifesto.

Attending the University of Chicago Booth School of Business changed my life in one significant way. I met my future husband there. We both did everything we could to avoid dating at school, but as I like to joke, the force of attraction was too strong. Our first date in fall 2011 sealed our fate, and things quickly got serious. I met his parents early in the relationship and still recall how his mother greeted me in her home with a warm hug while four cats darted about. Dating was romantic but intense, involving hard conversations that included our upbringing, religious views, value systems, political beliefs, children, and money.

Then in 2013, as we headed toward engagement, he asked a thought-provoking question while we were planning our lives together: "What do you think of the idea of living off the lower of our two incomes for the rest of our lives? We would never have to worry about the financial pressures of being parents or falling into the two-income household trap." My husband was primarily referencing the book *The Two-income Trap: Why Middle-class Parents Are Going Broke* by Elizabeth Warren, a former U.S. senator and onetime presidential candidate, and entrepreneur Amelia Warren Tyagi. The authors noted that while two-income households today earn more than single-income households of a generation ago, two-income households have less discretionary income to cover living costs because the cost of everything has risen significantly. The advantages of living on one income were obvious to me: Neither of us would have to fear unemployment. If we had kids, we could have the flexibility to take care of them longer than the typical parental leave granted by corporate America allows.

I was intrigued, but it sounded like a tall order. At the time, we were in a long-distance relationship, and I was getting ready to move to New York City to be with him—not exactly a cheap place for us to try out this fiduciary experiment. Plus, there were so many things I'd wanted as part of my grand plan, which did not include living in a cramped apartment or walking twenty blocks with groceries to avoid spending my entire paycheck at Whole Foods. I wanted a glamorous lifestyle like that portrayed by my business-school peers and my favorite TV drama, *Gossip Girl*. I wanted to carry an "it" handbag and wear beautiful heels. I wanted to show people that I had made it! I had worked so hard up until this point. Why would I want to go back to being as frugal as my parents were? I enjoyed eating out, going on trips to wine country, and playing with fashion. How would we make a single-income budget work? And all this is for imaginary children we might have in the future, and who knows when that would happen?

Our first year of marriage was a mess. I was trying to live off this new, extremely restrictive budget without really buying into *why* I was doing it; I had simply attributed it to my husband's desire to live cheaply. This bred a lot of resentment on my part and frustration on his. I needed money to eat out and make new friends in New York and to purchase the clothes and accessories I needed to look the part of the successful woman. To solve marital disputes, my husband suggested that we each have a discretionary allowance of $1,000 per year to spend, no questions asked; everything else in the budget had to be agreed upon. Soon afterward, a high-school friend asked me to be a bridesmaid at her wedding, and paying for the dress, the bachelorette party, and the wedding gift, I soon spent all of my "discretionary" budget. I struggled even to meet with colleagues for after-work drinks. When the Booth School of Business women's network held a social tea, the $60 entry fee was too much for me that month. I canceled and vented to my husband—again—that our restrictive budget was ruining my life.

I behaved erratically during this time, canceling on friends at the last minute or getting really stressed out about the cost of something. Because I hadn't told anyone about our arrangement, my friends didn't understand. I must have been talking my husband down a lot at the time as well, because most of my friends thought that I was having marital trouble. But I was doing all this because I was stubborn, and dang it, when I commit to a goal, no matter how ill-conceived it is, I will come at it with 110% effort because I had come to define myself by my work ethic and productivity.

Then I turned twenty-nine—a year that made me question everything I had lived for.

For years, I had played with the idea of being an entrepreneur or business owner. Mark Zuckerberg, the founder and CEO of Meta, was only one year older than I was, and if he could start his own company, then so could I! While exploring this career path, I came upon the *Forbes* "30 Under 30," the magazine's yearly it-list of thirty entrepreneurs under the age of thirty. Many of my friends from college had made it on that list. I became fixated on the idea that I needed to as well. No one put this idea in my head. It was a warped and incorrect conclusion I came to on my own because I had an overabundance of ambition that depended on others' validation.

In 2014, at age twenty-nine, I was still nowhere close to being named to the list. As dramatic as it seems in retrospect, I started to feel at the time like I didn't matter, that everything I'd worked for up to that point had been futile. I felt like a waste of breath, a waste of time, a waste of emotions. Nothing I did was ever good enough for my bosses. I was working at the leading lingerie company in the world, in a work culture where your total dedication and loyalty went above your own personal needs—not uncommon in the fashion industry. I often burst into tears at home, even in front of a guest or two, after particularly difficult days. When I tried to get time off to attend my friend's wedding, I was told by my supervisor that it wasn't possible. But I couldn't miss it, so I left the office, packed my laptop so I could work on the road, and forwarded my phone. However, I missed a phone call from my boss, and upon returning to the office, I received multiple lectures and was called "manipulative." One of my bosses asked why I felt I needed to go to the wedding. When I answered that it was important for me to be there for my friend, she said dismissively and emphatically that she missed her own wedding anniversary when work got intense, and she would do it again in a heartbeat.

I desperately wanted to change my bosses' perception of me. I wanted to keep my job, and I wanted to get better at it. But some of the pieces of the work grind didn't fit me. Having attended many networking events about "being a woman in the corporate world," I found they all centered on this point: When you become a mother, your career will inevitably be impacted, possibly forever, and it is unlikely that you'll ever reach the C-suite as quickly as a man or a child-free woman would. However, with the support of a veritable army of staff—nannies, night nurses, and babysitters—one can still make that CEO dream happen. I was appalled that this was the conclusion each time, whether it was an alumnae gathering or a conference with hundreds of female executives. My fellow Booth and Harvard classmates nodded and wrote this down in their corporate-branded Moleskine notebooks which they would later tuck into their Louis Vuitton Neverfull totes. The message was that I needed to be like Sheryl

Sandberg, who famously returned to work soon after having her first child and checked emails while her newborn napped. I had to "lean in."

It was then that I started to feel like I was hurling toward the wrong destination. If I continued down the path of my high-school manifesto, I would always be subject to the judgment of others. They would define who I was. If I wanted to be a CEO, my performance would be measured by shareholders, who would be many times more unforgiving about my personal life than my bosses in fashion. If I were to take my cues from Sandberg and hire multiple nannies, I would be just as absent and cold and tiger-like as my parents had been with me. The level of perfection I wanted to reach depended too much on external factors—and there was a high likelihood that I would never be happy. If I needed the world to validate me, magazines to write about me, bosses to like me, friends to admire me... what would happen if I stopped working? If I got injured in an accident and lost my ability to work or earn? Where would I find my own value and self-worth then?

The God I believe in would say, "Of course Shang has value, regardless of what she does." Everything about my life up to this point had been judged by some external entity, and I needed that affirmation to feel like I mattered. And yet, the more I tried to achieve those goals, the more unhappy, unfulfilled, and depressed I became. I'd stopped attending church and rarely prayed unless I wanted or needed something from God. Somewhere along the way, I had become cold and transactional, measuring friendship by whether a person would be beneficial to my career—a stark contrast to the warm and loving mother I wanted to be when I eventually had children of my own.

On the other hand, my husband, who was subject to similar stresses as I experienced, always seemed joyful and grounded. He wasn't impressed by the same panache that attracted me to New York's glitterati. He could be satisfied at any level of income or living standard. Like any other person, he could be affected by what others said about him, but it didn't reduce him to a puddle of sadness. Since we are often the products of our childhood, I began wondering: How could I be like his parents, who attended all his softball games and said "I love you" every day they saw him? How could I raise children who are resilient, not anxious and high-strung, who could thrive in the face of any challenge and be positive influences on the world?

Like the comedian Ali Wong famously declared in her debut Netflix show, *Baby Cobra*, I found myself wanting to lie down instead of lean in. Peace out. Sayonara, corporate suckers! The entire childhood dream I'd built up in my angsty diary pages crumbled before my eyes as I experienced this identity crisis. To lean *out*, to be the kind of loving parents that we wanted to be, to build a beautiful home life that honored God and each other, we needed financial independence. Not to be rich, but to be flexible. Money was a tool we could use to buy ourselves options and freedom, not a measure of our worth as human beings. The option I wanted to execute upon becoming a mother was to give a big middle finger to the appalling lack of maternity-leave policies in the United States and gift myself the luxury of having as much as a whole year off as a first-time mom. Once my north star realigned to this new goal, I wanted to escape my toxic situation. So I doubled down and bought into the extreme frugal lifestyle. More of the how-to will come later in the book, but it was by committing to this idea—that every cent we didn't spend would go toward purchasing our freedom—that we were able to save a mind-boggling 50% of our pre-tax income and put that into the stock market.

One day, a friend told me I should read Mr. Money Mustache, one of the earliest blogs that popularized the idea of "financial independence, retire early," or FIRE, via extreme frugality. Reading the MMM blog was the first time I ever felt understood for what I was trying to do, even though early retirement wasn't my desire. I just wanted a year to lie down without wrecking my career. In 2017, I began my own blog, Save My Cents, to share with others our financial experiences and what I learned. I didn't realize how much joy I would get from coaching and teaching others the lessons I had learned myself. A few years later, through the miracle of in-vitro fertilization, our children arrived, in 2019 and 2022. After delivering my second child, I had a severe health scare that landed me in the ICU for a day. I remember laugh-crying to the social worker that I didn't want to die and was shocked when they told me the person in the room right across the hall was dying. It shook me to my core. It made me question many of my life choices even more than I had already. I realized I didn't have the burning desire to return to my corporate job at a Fortune 500 health-care company. My colleagues didn't seem to care about me. My boss misspelled my son's name on the birth announcement to the team and didn't blink an eye when I told her I was in the ICU. It was like 2014 at the lingerie company all over again, except almost ten years had passed and I was much more financially established. Shang, I told myself, you have enough money to walk away from all of this. Don't wait for another sign.

It took a near-death experience for me to finally surrender my high-school manifesto and walk away. This "rich" life I had originally imagined as the ultimate act of revenge against my bullies and a way to earn love wasn't what I actually wanted. I told my boss I wanted to write a book, spent a few minutes firing off goodbye emails, and then went to the Walt Disney Concert Hall in Los Angeles to watch Gustavo Dudamel conduct the Los Angeles Philharmonic—my first foray into the realm of ladies who lunch, wear pearls and diamonds, and attend yoga classes at 10:30 a.m. For the rest of 2023 and much of 2024, I got to live my life's dream—to pursue something I'd called a passion project my entire life, a mission worthy of the time I had willingly donated to soulless Fortune 500 companies—write this book. You might not believe it right now, but anyone with a sound mind and body reading this book can change the future of their finances. That's why I wrote this book. Anyone. Including you.

You might be thinking, There is no way that could be true. That's not me. I didn't come from wealth. My parents were terrible with money. I only saw debt. I'm bad at math. I'm not smart enough. I only saw my parents saying, "There will never be enough money." I will show you how to begin healing those feelings and truly transform your financial future. I want you to believe that you can be successful with personal finance, and I'll be here to guide you. I'm here to help change and heal your money story.

As you read *Wealth Is a Mindset*, you will see that I cover many financial topics. I designed this book so that the earlier chapters address more beginner-level financial topics and progress toward the more advanced topics at the end. The goal of this book is to give you the inspiration and the courage you need to begin or renew your personal finance journey, with a focus on your mindset. I'm going to show how your childhood and your current situation all impact how you behave. I will teach you some valuable skills to help change your thinking so that you feel less anxious and fearful about your money. I will teach you not just budgeting and personal finance math, but actual brain-healing activities grounded in neuroscience and psychology to help you transform your money life, cent by cent. Once you learn to change your mind, everything else follows. I expect that if you commit to what I teach in this book, you will save more money, pay off more debt, increase your income, invest more money, and eventually gain more wealth and financial freedom.

CHAPTER ONE

IT'S NOT JUST THE NUMBERS

Feeling Shamed by My Budget

When my husband and I got married in 2013, one of the first things we did was immediately merge our finances. Our goal was to eventually reach financial freedom so that neither of us would ever fear for our livelihoods if and when we took parental leaves to care for our much-hoped-for future children. To achieve financial freedom, we agreed that we would drastically reduce our living expenses and live off the lower of our two incomes to fast-track our way there. We lived a life best described by financial writers at the time as FIRE—Financial Independence, Retire Early.

The tenet of FIRE rests on extreme frugality and is promoted by the likes of Mr. Money Mustache and Vicki Robin's *Your Money or Your Life*, and Kristy Shen and Bryce Leung's *Quit Like a Millionaire*. In essence, one purchases financial freedom in the future by living frugally today, sometimes to measures considered extreme by most people. Some FIRE pursuers downsize to living with their parents, in trailers, or small homes or ADUs. Others simplify their meals to the basic macronutrients and repeatedly eat the same thing day in, day out. Many keep few possessions, avoid car ownership, wear clothing until it gets riddled with holes, and relish in picking up free items from the curb on trash day. A commonality among FIRE adherents is to be very analytical in their thinking. After all, you need to use math to understand how your investments can grow to sustain your annual expenses.

FIRE happens when you meet the 4% Rule: when 4% of your net worth is equivalent to your annual expenses.[1] Many people pursuing FIRE even calculate an estimated FIRE date and often share their progress on social media. From what I've seen, the vast majority of FIRE pursuers also have high-paying jobs that make good use of their love of math, working in fields such as software engineering, finance, and management consulting.

I had just turned twenty-eight when I moved to New York City in 2013, leaving a well-paid tech job and a loyal group of friends in San Francisco. Since I hadn't started a full-time job yet in New York, I had the time to furnish my husband's and my starter 420-square-foot apartment so we could stop sleeping on an air mattress. As a FIRE pursuer, I was to do all this as cheaply as possible.

There wasn't much yet in the apartment. My husband brought a chair and shoe rack; I contributed some kitchen utensils. The previous tenants left behind a large stuffed couch and a fake Roy Lichtenstein painting on the wall. Our bedroom was just large enough for a full-sized bed, so I found someone selling the right bed frame and a mattress for just $50 on Craigslist.[2] I knew that buying a used bed was risky business, bedbugs and all. However, the seller claimed to be an investment banker who rarely slept at home, so how bad could it be?

I knew I couldn't move the bed by myself, and a professional moving company was out of the budget. Another search on Craigslist yielded a man with a van company who could help me move this bed set twenty blocks from the seller to our apartment. One hot summer day, I met two bulky men driving an unmarked white van at the seller's apartment. As I started for the door, I noticed only one of the two men following me.

"What about your partner?" I asked the person following me.

"Him? You didn't hire him."

"What do you mean?"

"You doing the $45-an-hour deal, yeah? That's *one* man with a van. If you want two men with a van, that's extra. You should be paying $75-an-hour for that. He's just watching the van for us."

You can't be serious, I thought. I was getting swindled on one of my first weeks after arriving in this city! A flush of anger quickly rose, and I had to stop myself from responding with some choice words. I thought to myself, What was the worst that could happen if I tried carrying half the weight, since one mover was here anyway? If I got tired halfway through, then I'd just pay for the other mover at that point. You never know if you can do it until you try, right? In retrospect, it makes total sense to pay for more labor, but at the time all I could think about was how the extra expense was not expected nor budgeted for.

We loaded the bed quickly into the van, and I rode in the back because I didn't feel like waiting or paying for the subway. During that short ride to our apartment, I shed tears as I texted the ridiculousness of the situation to my husband. It had come down to needing to save money, and I couldn't even afford the second man whom I thought I'd hired! I was definitely not starting out my life in New York City with a bang. With great effort and breaking a real sweat, I eventually moved the bed up the stairs with just one of the movers. I panted and sweated and asked for a break midway. Eventually, the mover felt bad and shifted more of the weight onto his shoulders.

Afterward, I closed the door and slumped onto the barely used mattress. (At least the seller was honest about its condition because it looked brand new.) I briefly felt triumphant that I had carried the bed, but those feelings quickly gave way to an hours-long session of me stewing in shame, anger, and indignation over not being able to afford two movers. The thing was, no one else had witnessed what had happened. Why did I feel shame then? The two men moving the van would forget me by their next gig and probably laugh about me as the silly customer that day who decided to do half their job for them. Why did it bother me so much? Was it because this was not the New York City life I imagined for myself? Because the movers weren't kind? Because I couldn't find the voice to argue? Because I appeared cheap?

Shortly after creating our new budget, I wrote to my husband: *I'm driven to tears every day thinking of our extremely frugal budget, and I just want it to stop.*

We're debt free. I got a job in less than three months. I never liked this budget. I don't agree with it. I hate how poor it makes me feel. I'm miserable. I'm disgruntled, unhappy, jealous, and all of those things and more.

Notice how I used the word "poor," even though by all measures, I was not in any way a person living in poverty. I felt very emotional with money and was letting my feelings override the facts. What I was actually feeling was *shame*— shame that I, someone who was accomplished at work, was now limited in my actions. I felt isolated in that I couldn't "keep up" with my classmates and their social lives. The media had me believe that a wealthy person looks like someone who spends a lot of money, and I didn't look like what wealthy people looked like on TV. I was doing something very different that made me stand out, just like how I was different in my passion to succeed as a child, which made me a target for bullying. I didn't want to feel rejected by society again.

At that point, my husband and I were just at the beginning of our careers. Financial freedom seemed like an unrealistic, far-off future possibility. Why not just enjoy what we made now so that we didn't stick out and risk getting laughed at by others? While we were in a brownstone over a hundred years old, most of our friends lived in shiny skyscraper condos with elevators and uniformed doormen. While I had sweated in the back of a van, my classmates would have just called a cab. I had worked so hard in school and in previous jobs that I felt I should be able to afford the same lifestyle as that of my friends, but I didn't see anyone else with a similar of background making the financial choices I was making. I was lost in my perception of the world around me, as well as in my fear of being ridiculed.

I was so busy comparing myself to the "should have" and "supposed to be" that I let in feelings of jealousy, want, and comparison. I put myself into a scarcity mindset and believed that I mattered less than others because my life didn't appear as perfect as I had imagined. By association, the feelings of shame I had also led to my reliving the bullying I had experienced in my childhood, which further magnified my fear of being mocked by others. At the time, I didn't appreciate just how high a goal my husband and I had set together. I needed a mindset and approach to life that were *unlike anything* I'd seen in media and demonstrated by my friends up to that point. To get into that wealthy mindset, it wasn't my budget that needed fixing. It was my mental health.

When Budgets Don't Work

In 2017, when I first started Save My Cents with the aim to change people's lives one cent at a time, I measured the rate at which my clients could keep to a few preidentified metrics for success. One of them was tracking their expenses on time once a month. I checked in regularly with my clients using an Excel sheet I designed that showed their actual spending, by category, compared with what we'd budgeted to spend that month. By my own measures, my clients succeeded half the time in sticking to their budgets. Whenever I didn't hear back from someone about their budget, I would hang my head in shame and frustration, feeling that I must have failed them somehow. I was already a seasoned business owner at that point, but if my clients didn't find success, then that told me what I was setting out to do was not working. What went wrong?

Creating a budget is one of the very first steps that most personal finance books will tell you to do when it comes to money. Every year, these books hit the shelves and promise that if you follow their steps, you can get out of debt, build some savings, and have financial freedom. But first, you have to budget. That's how I began as a personal finance coach too—with budgets. And that was my big mistake.

What is a budget? A *budget* is a plan for your money, usually in the form of a table or a spreadsheet. There's often a space at the top where you write how much money you make, then you subtract for a specific period of time how much you spend from that amount. If you spend more than you planned to spend, you may end up dipping into your savings and owing a debt. If you spend less than you planned, you have money to save and put in reserve. When attempting to budget, most people do so to avoid going into debt.

In 2016, at age thirty-one, I had already finished saving for retirement, primarily through extreme frugal living combined with a job that paid six figures. I felt giddy and was living off the high of my accomplishment when I decided to launch a small, low-fee personal finance coaching business. I still had my full-time job, so this business was mostly experimental and meant to last for just a short time. My goal was to help people accelerate their ability to save money and invest; at the time, this meant to help my clients budget. It seemed like a straightforward, black-and-white concept. All I had to do was show people how much they could save each month and which categories they could pare back in spending. If they spent less than we budgeted, we celebrated. If they spent more, we still celebrated any progress but would dig into what went wrong. By following these simple steps, I thought my clients would get rich, pay off their debts, and live without worrying about money. Isn't that what everyone wants? Wouldn't it be fantastic? I could change lives without ever having to become the heart surgeon my immigrant parents initially hoped I would become!

I was also pretty naïve. I didn't realize that my plan was the personal finance equivalent to skipping the ABCs and jumping straight to cramming Charles Dickens into people's brains.

Among my first batch of coaching clients were various people who, on paper, appeared well-off. Many made six-figure incomes like I did, but had much higher expenses, with discretionary spending concentrated in areas like apparel and accessories, eating out and socializing, and beauty. Most of my clients were aware that they were spending more than they'd like to and struggled with reining in their expenses. While I was busy with budgeting, I began observing the connections between my clients' mindsets and how that impacted their financial wellness. I'll provide two of these clients as examples.

One client whom I'll call Alice did a fantastic job submitting her budgeting homework. She was never late and responded promptly, which, to me as a coach, meant that she had a high level of commitment to the goal of reducing her expenses and becoming financially free. Alice struggled mostly with her spending on self-care. She spent hundreds of dollars per month on hair, nails, and clothing. On top of that, there were unplanned movies and other forms of entertainment. Thankfully, Alice made a lot of money to afford it all, but that meant she had less savings than she wanted. We got on a call to discuss my analysis of her budget, and she shared a crucial piece of information that would become one of the defining moments of how I would later help people organize their finances.

Alice bravely made herself vulnerable with me right at the beginning of our working relationship and told me she had clinically diagnosed depression.

On the surface, I saw a successful lawyer making six figures, living in a dreamy California destination. But beneath the cover was a disease that was beyond my comprehension. Depression ate away at her and made it very difficult for her to commit to things, and also caused her to have anxiety. Alice shared that spending money allowed her to feel in control and self-soothe when her disease got the better of her. In essence, money was a way to comfort her when she wanted immediate relief from her symptoms.

Since I'm not a psychologist, I immediately realized this was a situation I wasn't trained to handle appropriately. I felt as if I were working against a mental disease that I had no idea how to overcome; all I felt I could do was hope that Alice's prescribed medicines and talk therapy worked for her. I identified areas where she could save more money, but in the end we eased up on the push to lower her spending and agreed she would just do her best. Alice was one of my first clients, but certainly not the last, where her money story was not just about simply reducing expenses and investing the difference. She wasn't even the most difficult case because she had savings.

The other client who made a big impact on me in those early months was Wendy, a single mother of two children. Wendy worked as a wedding photographer in New England. She would've been financially secure if it weren't for the fact that she had an incredible amount of student loan debt. After college, she was briefly married and had her first child. She went to graduate school, but unfortunately her child became very sick right when Wendy had to write her final thesis and pass her exams. The financial aid department told her she didn't qualify for more aid, so she took on debt to finish school. Wendy never made enough money to make a significant dent in her debt, and her ex-husband didn't pay enough in child support for her and her child's living to be comfortable. Her divorce and custody battle added another $25,000 to her loan balance.

By the time I was helping Wendy, her loans totaled six figures and she had entered into a "debt relief" program that was overcharging her for what they were doing without really giving her relief.[3] Despite Wendy's best efforts at tracking her expenses dutifully with me for over a year and my encouraging her to find higher-paying photography gigs, her debt didn't seem to be lessening. She constantly went over the budget I'd suggested, and I couldn't tell where the money was going, as it was often labeled "vitamins" and "other." Wendy didn't appear to be overspending on the basics—she cooked as much as she could and didn't buy a lot of new clothes. She simply had little margin for error. If she suffered even one emergency, she added more to her debt.

Years later, Wendy finally broke up with her then boyfriend and admitted to me that he was a cheater who struggled with alcoholism and made everything about himself. I learned that the entire time I was trying to help her, she wasn't putting herself first. Her life revolved around trying to save her boyfriend, tending to his needs, crossing her own boundaries to the point where she stopped giving herself a much-needed break. Looking back, there were so many signs of his negative involvement in her life, but at the time I didn't see them or add them together. She was enduring so much beyond what I could see on the spreadsheet, and I had no idea. Some of her decisions around her finances were likely due to the fact that she was overwhelmed and wasn't in a position to care for herself. Had I taken a little more time to get to know what was happening with her boyfriend, I perhaps could have made the whole process a little smoother. Neither Wendy nor I would have given up as quickly as we did, and we probably could have made better progress together.

You Are Not a Number

You might have started budgeting at some point in your life. Maybe you've even read a few books or articles about personal finance. Most will teach you how to budget by calculating your income, expenses, and goals, and I'll do that too. However, before we get there, let's make something abundantly clear: You are not just a set of numbers on a page.

Open up YouTube or any celebrity gossip page on any given day, and you'll find many videos and articles discussing famous people and their net worth. Every year, publications create lists of people who have "made it" in their fields before ages thirty, thirty-five, and forty, as if anyone over forty is entering the encyclopedia of obsolescence (in fact, I turn forty the year this book releases). The media is obsessed with the drama of tech billionaires like Elon Musk and Mark Zuckerberg, and divorces make a celebrity's finances painfully public, like that of Amazon founder Jeff Bezos. From Zillow, you can easily find out how much a celebrity's house is worth. On LinkedIn, you can see your professional connections announce new job titles, promotions, products they launch, and conferences they attend. All these posts hint at worldly success and are defined by numbers, and when it's published somewhere public, it's easy to assume that is all there is to the story. The numbers, without context, feel cold, unapproachable, out of reach, and judgmental. *It's no wonder that personal finance does not feel personal.* The narrative focuses on your career, spending, debt, and income. It's all numbers, no humanity.

Your money story is deep-rooted. It's about more than just what you make and spend. It includes stories as personal and specific as the time you didn't get a birthday gift you hoped for, or the time you snuck into the kitchen before bed and saw your mother shedding tears over a stack of bills. It includes the moment you toted precious possessions in a small suitcase as you left home for a smaller apartment somewhere else. Or maybe it includes the time you waited for your father to return home after a long day at work with small treats for you to eat. Some people's money stories begin with working in the family restaurant, mopping floors, cleaning dishes, translating documents from the bank for their immigrant parents, and taking orders on the phone.

Growing up in Massachusetts, I was convinced we were a low-income household. I remember my dad beaming when he bought a bright green used car from a no-name car manufacturer. "We got a good deal," he said. "Remember that this color saved us a lot of money!" My mother had the newspaper open all the time to clip coupons for Macy's and Filene's, and she knew the prices of milk and eggs at the local grocery stores. Even as a teenager, I myself understood the value of a dollar. I'd note that a box of eighteen Gobstoppers cost $0.75 each at a specialty candy store, while a box of forty-two Gobstoppers cost $0.42 each at CVS. I knew my parents paid dearly for piano lessons for me at the New England Conservatory Preparatory School, where I first came in contact with really wealthy people. The kids attended private schools, went on international vacations, and always wore new shoes. I thought I was just the public-school kid who was lucky to be there. And since so much money was spent on my lessons, I was determined to make them worth it by winning nearly all the piano competitions I entered, accumulating medals and trophies that we barely had enough space for in the house.

As I entered adolescence, my parents often made remarks and threats like, "If you don't get into Harvard or MIT, you will pay for everything yourself," so I had always assumed I would have to pay for my own college tuition. But when I started applying to schools, my parents told me not to bother applying for financial aid. "What do you mean, don't bother? Don't I need to fill it out to see if I get any financial aid for college?" I asked. My father then revealed that he'd been investing toward my college tuition for years. In fact, he had enough investments to send me with room and board to any school my heart desired. I felt like a deer in headlights, not knowing how to react. I was happy that I wouldn't have to take on loans, but also very confused why they kept this information from me until now. Maybe this was just another quirk of their parenting style; at least, that was how I reasoned it to be at the time. Having my education fully funded is a privilege most people don't get, and I am proud of and grateful to my parents for making the sacrifices and strategic financial decisions to get our family to that position.

This is just part of my money story, but on paper, all this would usually be summed up in numbers. What about how I grew up? What about the surprise I felt that my college tuition would be completely covered? How do you quantify all of that into a budget? You can't. You live it. You experience it. You see, hear, and sometimes even recall just by scent alone. (For me, the smell of vinegar always brings me back to my first college job, which involved mopping floors and cleaning dorm bathrooms.) Your money story encompasses so much, and it's also found in what is not spoken. Most people can describe whether their childhood was comfortable, but few know whether it was due to their parents being wealthy or spending from debt. In cases of bankruptcy or financial difficulty, parents are usually loathe to share the reality with their children because they feel so much shame and don't know how to talk about it.

This richness is what I was missing when I first began coaching Alice and Wendy. I didn't fully appreciate how much someone's money story would manifest in actions and behaviors well into adulthood. Whereas most personal finance education centers around teaching you how money works, I want to go back to those first memories and encounters with money. I want to dive into what made you who you are today, draw out your strengths, and help you find closure and peace over areas of your life where you may feel shame. These are the parts where the numbers don't reveal everything. A person could go thousands of dollars in debt from buying one luxury item just as easily as they could from incurring medical bills for an emergency operation. That debt sitting in your statements doesn't say anything on its own; it's the circumstances and personal choices that led to the bill that tell the full story. Don't let your money shame you, because your money story is more than just numbers. And it's also okay to want more of it! Money is simply a tool and doesn't have to be a bad or evil thing. I once jokingly quipped on a speaking panel, "Money is like a knife. Use it poorly, and it can kill you. Use it well, and it can feed you." I still believe that to be true. We have to start with your dreams and goals because if you don't want to change your life, then nothing I do will help.

Once Wendy finally recognized that it was okay for her to want wealth for herself, she began doubling down on investing in herself. She found ways to make more money by trying out new styles of photography, riding a social media wave that elevated lifestyle photography. With her extra earnings, she began putting savings away for a rainy day and for her children. She learned how to invest and speak my love language—low-cost, diversified stock funds! (You'll learn more about these later in the book.) Wendy decided that she never wanted a relationship as toxic as her alcoholic ex. She paid a lot for a life coach, but it was a wise financial decision as she learned to work on her own needs and eventually became more confident in herself and her capabilities. She started dating someone who treasured her, honored her, and made her feel important and loved. Her desire to improve her life and make more money gave her the courage to change parts of her life so that she could reach her goals. She saw herself as a person whose goals are worthy of pursuing. When I last spoke to Wendy, her voice radiated with hope, strength, and joy.

So, do you want to change your life? Do you want it more than air, more than your last meal, more than anything else? Because when you want to change your life, then changes in your money story become inevitable. No matter how you feel about money, it impacts everything. One day, it may be possible that you will reach your dreams because you decided today that you want to change your money story.

Wealth Is a Mindset

In the years following, I began shifting my focus to mindsets instead of budgets. In particular, I realized that some people have a scarcity mindset while some people have an abundance mindset, which can affect their finances and overall lifestyle. People with a scarcity mindset fear that life is unlikely to work out, that their financial outlooks appear to be grim and limited, and as a result, they often make decisions around money that limit their potential. People with an abundance mindset think the opposite. They often see their income-earning potential as unlimited and view failures as temporary setbacks rather than permanent obstacles, and thus are more likely to succeed in changing their money story.

Once I understood a person's money story encompassed more than what the numbers covered, I realized I needed to know people's histories and how they thought about money before I could help them transform their lives financially. Rather than lead with a budget spreadsheet, I identified whether a client was holding scarcity or abundance in their minds. If they were holding thoughts of scarcity, then it would not be telling them how to change their budget; instead, it would be to help them move away from the fears that were holding their minds captive. This change led to so much success for my clients that one of them in turn has wholly inspired me in my own life and approach to coaching. Maria gives a very realistic example of what it takes to turn one's financial life around through a change in mindset.

Maria was twenty-nine years old, a single mother to a toddler child. She carried the weight of the world on her shoulders. She followed me on social media for about a year before she finally reached out: "Hi Shang! I am ready to commit to receiving your expert help! The only way I knew I would be ready was when I finally   sold my dream car I bought two years ago! Well, as of today, my car is sold! This means to me, mentally, I am ready to start taking my future with my baby girl seriously!" Her parents didn't have much in retirement savings, and Maria was determined to evolve her money story and do something very different with her life. Her dream was to pay off her debt, invest in her retirement, and have a better life for her daughter.

Maria's parents were not wealthy in terms of actual money but rich in love for their children. They spent a lot each year on family trips, amusement parks, and going out. In her adulthood, her family pressured her to chip in for expensive birthday parties, takeout, and other indulgences that, quite frankly, she couldn't afford on a single income with a child to feed. As a result, Maria racked up credit card and student loan debt. She managed to pay off her credit card before meeting me. However, while paused due to government intervention during the COVID-19 crisis, student loans still presented an obstacle to her dream of building wealth and retiring comfortably. Maria admits, "My parents were always good at saving their money for a rainy day, but they did not save for their retirement. Because of the way I was brought up, I prioritized spending and shopping and traveling... over saving for retirement."

As I coached Maria, I focused on her family's belief that proof of a good life was spending a lot of money. I discussed with her how it was possible to be a fantastic daughter, sister, and family member without lavishly spending on her family, and gave her a plan that placed that dynamic front and center. But a few months into the plan, Maria still struggled. She had paid for an pan international trip that was completely unplanned but she felt pressured by her family to go on. She also hinted at conflicts at home. Finally, eighteen months after we first started working together, Maria pushed herself to a monumental decision: She would finance a $40,000 car, leave her parent's home, and strike it out alone. While it was not the most optimal choice, she recognized that she needed to move out to preserve her own mental health. Her father flew into a rage upon discovering she was moving out, and her siblings didn't express strong support for her decision either. She was under immense pressure and shame from all sides.

The move meant a drastic increase in her monthly spending—her rent went up, she now had a significant car payment, and she had almost no wriggle room financially. However, after she moved out, for the first time since I'd gotten to know her, I heard glimmers of hope and joy in our exchanges. She relished the simplicity of eating homemade food with her daughter instead of takeout for dinner. She began seeing all her possessions as good enough and felt less need to spend more. Peace returned to her voice.

I'll return to Maria's story throughout the book because it shows how the journey to save more money and invest it for an uncertain future is very mental. The stronger one's mind, the easier it gets. Often it can take years for us to look back on our struggles and understand what we have to do to get through them. In the beginning, fear may take over, especially if one doesn't know how to go from a scarcity mindset—"I am scared"—to an abundance mindset—"Do it scared." We dismiss tried-and-true tactics because our brains are too burned out and overloaded to set aside the time to breathe and see the bigger picture. Remember, the mind is our most powerful organ. What we tell it and what it believes manifest in real-life outcomes. To change our lives and our money stories, we need to change our minds. Thankfully, there are tangible ways to do that.

CHAPTER TWO

YOUR MONEY AND YOUR BRAIN

"It feels good to know that someone can see and understand how I truly feel. I read your emails over and over again and they make me cry and feel a sense of relief and great sadness. The way you support me in this journey makes me feel like I CAN DO THIS."

This is what Maria wrote to me when we had our first breakthrough. We had been working together for over a year, but she still struggled with spending money, especially on her family and child. Over time, Maria began to open up and share more about how she and her family interacted. Trying to spend less money based on the advice I was giving her made her stand out among her family members. No one could understand what she was doing and why she was bowing out of some of their lavish parties. Because her family often disparaged her financial situation, Maria mentioned multiple times that her mental health suffered whenever she was around them, and she seemed happier now that she was living away from them. Still, Maria felt overwhelmed and alone, which was why she relied so much on hearing affirmation from me. No one else agreed with the lifestyle choices she was making, and none of her family understood what it took to build the kind of financial peace that Maria was seeking.

It is astounding how much taboo still surrounds the topic of mental health, even though people have become much more open about it in the past decade. When it comes to personal finance, people's mental state is still largely ignored. By not discussing our mental health, we miss out on perhaps the most significant and lasting way to change our lives—by addressing our minds. If we acknowledge the link between our mental health and our financial health, perhaps we can show more compassion for people who experience financial struggles. It's time to get to the root of how personal finance works: our brains.

In this chapter, I will take you through a brief scientific journey to help you understand how our brains and money habits work together. I'm not trying to replicate biology class, but learning about neuroscience and psychology can show why your money habits don't always feel like they're in your control. Sometimes the things we do with our money as adults stem from things that we experienced as babies or children. Bad financial outcomes are the symptoms, not the disease. Once you can see how your life has played out with the correlations scientists have discovered through research, you can dig into the source of your problems, make real changes, stop putting a Band-Aid on the problem, and heal real wounds. We will learn how our brains work, why we haven't adequately learned personal finance, and how painful experiences like poverty and adverse events can linger well into our adult lives.

Helpful Background Info

You don't need to know all the scientific information regarding how our brains and money habits are connected, and I know some of you want to get straight ahead to reading about personal finance tips! So, here are the key points that you need to know about the science:

- The skills required to manage money are executive-level functioning skills that engage the most complex reasoning part of our brain: the cortex.

- As children, we first learn to relate to the world through the lens of survival. Our first experiences are all coded emotionally into our memories.

- The current educational system in the United States does not adequately teach personal finance. Children who receive any instruction regarding personal finance are more likely to be better equipped to manage money as adults.

- Lower-income earners appear to make more short-term decisions with money, such as taking payday loans, because they suffer from a lack of time and energy. When exhausted and stressed, people don't think through a decision using the more complex cortex layer of their brains.

- There is a high correlation between low income and depression. Depression slows down our brains and makes decision-making more challenging, which makes personal finance functions, such as planning and thinking ahead, more difficult.

- A child who grows up with adverse events, such as an abusive environment, financial instability, and violence, is more likely to have the effects of these traumatizing memories follow them into adulthood, leading to health issues including depression, higher levels of smoking, and obesity.

- As adults, when we face situations that remind us of negative experiences from our childhood, we retreat to survival mode. These challenging circumstances often flood our brains with so many emotions that we may be unable to think clearly. The brain spirals into behaviors that mirror what we experienced as children. These episodes can lead to the accumulation of debt and the inability to increase personal wealth. That is why taking another look at our childhood is crucial in understanding how to change our adult financial behavior.

For the rest of this chapter, I will go into more detail about all the above points regarding the brain and its relationship to money. If you're curious to read more, I invite you to keep going. If you'd like to jump ahead to something that is more actionable, you are welcome to skip the rest of this chapter and go to Chapter Three.

The Three Systems of the Brain

According to research published in *Current Biology*, scientists believe that our brains evolved to have multiple layers, each controlling a group of similar functions. The inside layer is the reptilian system, the oldest system. Then comes the limbic system. Finally, there is the cortex, the layer that enables the complex reasoning that separates humans from other animal species.[4]

Our **reptilian** system controls the basics of living. This part of the brain ensures we're at the right body temperature of 98.6 degrees, regulates our heartbeat and breathing patterns, sends hunger signals when we've thoroughly digested our previous meal, and helps us stay safe. Most of the time, we don't even know that this system is actively working; if we did, our thoughts would overload.

The **limbic** system of our brain is the emotional system. It helps us process emotions, form and store memories, and encode those memories with emotions. When this part of the brain is injured or not functioning correctly, it often results in anxiety disorders, addiction, depression, and other complex neuropsychiatric disorders.

The **cortex** system is our most advanced system. I call it our computer because it controls thinking and advanced planning. When thinking, planning, making calculations, and absorbing new information, we engage the cortex part of our brain.

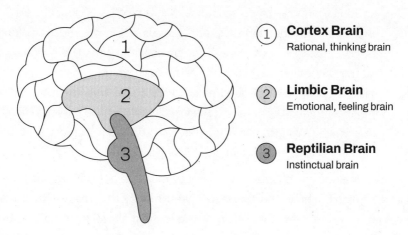

1. **Cortex Brain**
   Rational, thinking brain

2. **Limbic Brain**
   Emotional, feeling brain

3. **Reptilian Brain**
   Instinctual brain

When we are physically and mentally healthy, all systems of our brains work together as a team. The skills that are required to manage money well—

mathematics, planning, strategizing—are executive-level functions requiring the cortex system to be in tune, and our limbic system—the emotional side—to be working in harmony with it.

Child Brains Know Survival

Humans aren't born with an inherent understanding of how to manage money; we have to learn how to survive and stay alive. That's why our earliest memories as small children are often around survival and bonding. Kelsey Hunter, a behavior analyst at the Children's Hospital of Philadelphia, explains that children's brains aren't developed enough to understand complex topics, because one's cortex layer does not finish developing until they reach their mid-twenties. So, as we experience things for the first time, we assign them to one of four instinctual responses: fight, fright, freeze, or fawn.[5] These four responses are very important, especially when a situation is stressful, scary, or dangerous.[6]

Hunter says, "Our first exposure to finance and things like that are usually the most salient. It's your first experience with either having or not having a perceived need met, or a perceived want met, and it's speaking to a greater need." She shares that our child brains see things very simply: We have something, or we don't. There is no sense of planning for the future. Early childhood memories are encoded *emotionally*, using our limbic system. "Planning and decision-making...are skills that you learn, hone, and you get it over time. Emotional regulation—people seem to think that this is innate, but it actually has to be explicitly taught," Hunter explains.

While personal finance uses a lot of math, I found that when coaching my clients I was spending most of my time talking through their emotions and behavior. Certainly, a structured lesson on how to build a budget is also needed (we'll get to that), but addressing our feelings around money should come first because of how our brains are wired.

The US Education System Failed

According to the reports published by Nex Gen Personal Finance (NGPF), in 2019, just six states guaranteed that high schoolers would have a semester-long finance course as part of the requirements for graduation.[7] Yanely Espinal,

Director of Partnerships and Education Outreach at NGPF, explains, "Back in the day you had home economics. And students would learn how to budget for food and groceries and everyday life matters. But slowly, there were some criticisms of this class. Over time it got replaced by economics, macroeconomics. When NGPF first began offering free curriculum and free teacher training for teaching personal finance in schools, a lot of these teachers had never learned about how to manage money effectively themselves."

Thanks to the efforts of NGPF, as of November 2024, twenty-six states now implement some form of a finance course as part of the requirements for graduation, and sixteen other states are in process of doing so—an encouraging and growing trend. I hope that one day we will see this expand to all fifty states of the US because I don't remember learning anything about managing money in school.

Matt Walleart, a behavioral psychologist who worked on financial tech products, spoke to this problem as well. "I was head of product for a financial software company. The strongest people on the platform, i.e., those who chose to invest in their personal finance, were those following what their parents did. It can be parents explicitly teaching these practices to their children, but mostly I saw that it was the clients observing the actions passively. We see the strong influence of parental approaches to money. Both in actual behavior—like sitting down and budgeting, but also emotionally—whether parents get agitated or fight about money at home."

Anyone can step on a gas pedal and turn a steering wheel. Not everyone can drive safely without explicit instruction. Hence, we have mandatory driver's education classes to ensure everyone's safety on the road. Similarly, while anyone can swipe a credit card, it can be dangerous to give teenagers credit cards without teaching them how the cards work. Money is a life-or-death topic, but unfortunately, in the US, it's not treated as such by our educational system.

I attribute a considerable part of my financial success to my parents talking openly about money at home. I often heard juicy gossip about my extended family. Perhaps an uncle racked up some personal debt, my dad landed a grant that could bring more researchers to his lab, or an aunt was finally profitable in her latest business venture. My parents not only normalized money talk and made it part of our everyday lives, they also emphasized that there was no shame in living frugally. Though I perceived us to be low-income because my parents didn't splurge all that much, I didn't feel bad about it. I just thought that being frugal was the responsible thing to do. Growing up, I had no idea this experience around money was uncommon. When clients or peers first talk to me about personal finance, they often remark that they've never really learned how to approach it. In fact, a 2020 survey conducted by T. Rowe Price shows that 41% of parents are reluctant to discuss financial topics with their children![8] How can we expect people to know how to do something if we never talk about it?

No wonder we graduate into adulthood with few tools to learn how to approach personal finance. If you count the hours in school from kindergarten to twelfth grade, it amounts to over twenty-four thousand hours spent learning subjects ranging from math to reading to writing to history, but we have spent almost nothing on personal finance. That's a lot of time lost! It's something that is entirely not our fault, but it's frustrating to see that the system has failed us in such a fundamental way.

Brains Can't Decide When They're Sick

Why is it that lower-income earners use payday loans? These loans have ridiculously high interest rates (400% or more on an annualized basis), which keep the lower-income earners essentially indebted forever.

In their groundbreaking research on poverty and decision-making, professors Sendhil Mullainathan of Harvard University and Eldar Shafir of Princeton University looked into the psychology of scarcity, of not having enough. Their findings, summarized in their book, *Scarcity*, found that lower-income earners are not unintelligent or acting out of a lack of financial education; however, when someone doesn't have enough money or time to devote to anything other than survival, they may take actions that don't make logical sense. Lower-income earners are distracted, emotionally and mentally depleted, and hampered by past failures. When faced with financial difficulty, their brains can, in a sense, short-circuit, and they end up making decisions that hurt them in the long run. For example, they might put off a car repair that would help a car last longer. They don't delay this because of a lack of intelligence, but because they focus so much brainpower on simply existing that they don't have the capacity to think longer term, even if it is for their own benefit. They can't give their brains the time and energy required for a decision to run through the cortex layer and engage more strategic thoughts before they take action.

They're also more often depressed. Finances and mental health are so intertwined that it's difficult to tease out the causes and effects, but there are dozens of studies that show depression and financial stress are highly correlated.[9] Unemployment, low socioeconomic status, low education, and low income all contribute to depression, and there is also a high association between depression and anxiety and household financial stressors. It's difficult to say which comes first, but it's clear that these issues exist hand in hand and make it tough for people to make clear, long-term decisions. In a series of studies from 1999 to 2002, Robert L. Leahy, an expert on cognitive therapy, suggested that people with depression may try to avoid risk when making decisions. They may also tend to internalize feelings of regret, which can lead to inaction or avoidance.[10] Avoiding decisions can be devastating for wealth building. Because of depression, people might put off actions like taking better jobs, investing in income-producing assets, or trying to move on from perceived failures.

Nolan Zane, Professor Emeritus of Psychology and Asian American Studies and Director of the Asian American Center on Disparities Research at UC Davis, explains this more fully: "When people are clinically depressed, everything slows down. Not only do they move slower, they think slower. Even the simplest problem-solving issues and tasks that we take for granted during our daily routine, a clinically depressed person feels is a challenge and chore. Even thinking about what to do is painful. Common tasks like figuring out how much money you have in your bank, how can you financially plan, all get eroded away. Then it's really hard to get the people to the next level thinking of the future, how to save, how to think about retirement."

When I coach these days, I look for signs of depression and anxiety.[11] As logical and perhaps obvious as it may seem, my coaching clients are often amazed to find a strong connection between their mental and financial health and to realize it was there all along.

Adverse Childhood Events

How can highly successful, rational people suddenly do an about-face and end up making unusual and self-sabotaging decisions regarding their personal finance? It often goes back to core, defining moments in childhood. There is a considerable body of research that shows how negative memories from childhood can have lasting impacts on us as adults. From 1995 to 1997, the Centers for Disease Control and Prevention (CDC) and Kaiser Permanente conducted an adverse childhood experiences (ACEs) study with over seventeen thousand participants.[12] Examples of such memories included: emotional, physical, or sexual abuse; violence toward mothers; substance abuse; mental illness in the household; parental separation or divorce; incarcerated household members; and emotional or physical neglect. This study is considered one of the most extensive investigations of the impact of childhood abuse, neglect, and household challenges on later-life health and well-being.

Researchers found that if your childhood was dysfunctional, the resulting trauma tended to follow you into your adulthood, unless you made a concerted effort to process and heal from it. It seems obvious, but many adults cope in life by intentionally forgetting their childhood trauma or repressing or compartmentalizing it. The study confirmed that the more ACEs someone endured as a child, the more likely it could lead to smoking, severe obesity, physical inactivity, depressed moods, and suicide attempts. When we apply these correlations to the world of money, we see that those who had exposure to ACEs as children are less likely to be set up for success in managing their money as adults. Professor Zane summarizes that "this is the result of trauma, because trauma is a form of mental illness. Trauma is passed through generations, because the parents often don't deal with it as well as they should, they don't get mental health help. And that is why you see depression occur so commonly among people who grew up with trauma."

"Our bodies remember," behavioral analyst Kelsey Hunter adds. "If you have had lived-in stressful experiences, or you were in a physical state of stress and tenson... for example, children who have been exposed to challenges as a child, they might not remember the event anymore. But when exposed to a similar situation as an adult, they might have similar physical responses—sweaty hands, racing heartbeats, even phrases like, 'I don't know' or 'I don't care' or 'I'm just stupid.' And these are reactions that you don't even realize as such in the moment. This is a triggered response, not a learned response."

Why Your Brain Spins Out of Control

Daisy's parents divorced when Daisy was just two years old, so she spent her childhood being raised by her maternal grandparents and her mother. Money felt tight in both homes. Daisy's father had a substance abuse problem and spent some years in jail. From a young age, Daisy had traumatic experiences of seeing her father in jail, noticing her mother not having enough money to clothe her for school, and witnessing a high school friend overdose on drugs. Daisy never knew how to deal with these situations. The only time she remembered her mother happy was when her mother bought things.

After graduating from college, Daisy married an intelligent man with a master's degree. Unfortunately, her husband was very selfish and rarely put effort into their relationship and, eventually, their child. Daisy became the primary provider for their daughter and received no emotional support from her husband to care for her. As a result, Daisy tried to pay for everything with credit cards, not knowing whether there was enough money in the bank. She had no sense of control around money and spent impulsively. It got to the point where even basic necessities were adding to the credit card balance, and she defaulted to a state similar to what she saw growing up. After she separated from her husband, her anxiety hit the roof.

Daisy shared with me, "That's when everything felt so scary. People want immediate relief from their pain. That's why I'm dealing with the high credit card debt and unsure of how to move forward. It's this slow drip of childhood trauma, insecurity, not knowing how to do things, feeding impulses when I shouldn't. At that time, in therapy I would ask, 'Why do I feel so triggered? Why do I have all this anxiety? What went wrong?' I don't want this generational trauma to continue. It felt like there was no escaping. I can't keep hemorrhaging cash. I can't go further into debt."

What Daisy was describing was her inability to make sound decisions regarding money during her separation and divorce. In losing one of the most significant relationships of her life, she suffered immense amounts of emotional pain, with few people she could turn to. That agony was reminiscent of all the suffering she had felt as a child, and Daisy fell into a similarly dark and insecure place and relied on an old habit she observed from her mother: buying things as a way to happiness. By the time Daisy began working with me, it was almost three years after her divorce, and she was still struggling with her consumer debt.

If we don't learn how to cope with challenging situations as children or young adults, then like Daisy, we go into survival mode and tend to fall back on what we know. Any negative core memories and associated behaviors we have rear their ugly heads, possibly resulting in secondary trauma for those of us who have not had closure. Someone experiencing chronic stress is more likely to rely on old habits instead of working toward a long-term goal or taking on a new challenge.[13] When one is stressed, the cortex has more difficulty controlling and regulating the rest of the brain, including emotional reactions and survival instincts. The brain becomes deregulated. And when survival mode kicks in, the cortex, the part that is rational and thinks ahead, is not being engaged. Survival mode does not engage the part of our brain that is rational and thinks ahead. And that is why our finances often become ruined during these periods of stress.

"When we are anxious or depressed, we are no longer able to do long-term thinking," Hunter says. "Those adverse childhood experiences affect our brain development. When you have anxiety, your amygdala is overactive, it is constantly firing. This creates emotional exhaustion. The amygdala takes blood from our prefrontal cortex—the part of our brain that is making long-term decisions. You're now being 'flooded,' and with your amygdala firing, you're in fear, and you are no longer able to make decisions. You react more impulsively."

I work with many highly educated people with stable jobs, who own homes and cars, and their lives seem perfectly fine on the surface. Some of my clients make much more money than I ever did at the height of my career. But when faced with a financial challenge, they suddenly freeze or panic. They make irrational decisions around money and get stuck in this fear- and anxiety-induced spiral where all they feel is shame. These clients know intellectually that they are able to improve their money habits, but many don't want to see or refuse to admit how much debt they have. They're exhausted. Life is not joyful.

Every day feels incredibly draining, and it becomes difficult for them to think a few steps ahead because they are flooded with other concerns.

Your Story Matters

When someone approaches me at the height of their money troubles, a shortcut or a temporary solution won't change their lives in the long run. As you can see from everything I have discussed in this chapter, how you manage your money now as an adult is connected to your mental health and your childhood traumas and triggers. You need a healthy, functioning brain where all three systems work together. If you have depression, anxiety, or other mood disorders, they may interfere with your ability to make executive decisions and plan for your long-term future. If you experienced abuse or trauma in childhood, you likely carry that with you as an unhealed wound into adulthood and may react impulsively with your money when you enter a flooded or triggered state. What happened during your formative childhood years is where we need to begin so that we can understand how to heal you as an adult.

CHAPTER THREE

THE SOLUTION TO YOUR MONEY PROBLEMS

I'll let you in on a secret. If you read to the end of this chapter and skip the rest of the book, you will still have learned the most important thing I can teach you to change your money life. Excited? Heck yes! Changing your life should excite you and make you feel hopeful! It should also be simple. And guess what? It doesn't involve a budget—at least not right away. Phew, no need to dig up your old math textbooks!

However, simple does not mean easy. When you try to change your life, you may not feel happy at first. You might cry, feel lonely, and get frustrated as you transition. You might not know whom to talk to because few others seem to understand what you are doing. You might feel a lot of shame and regret about your past. This is all normal and part of the process, and it doesn't mean that you're broken or beyond help. In some ways, I need you to lean into the scary belief that things can and do work out. That if you commit to changing your life, it will eventually look different from how it does today, slowly but surely. I can't guarantee overnight success because I don't think that kind of change is necessarily sustainable, but I can say that with many of my clients, they start feeling more positively toward money, more secure, in as little as a month or two once they internalize what I will teach you.

To begin, let's first find out which money problem root causes you may have. Then, I will give you specific solutions to some of your top struggles. Even if you don't read the rest of the book and instead just put in some effort to implement the simple solution in this chapter, I guarantee you will see changes in your finances and in your life.

Three Root Causes of Money Problems

Beginning in 2021, I revamped my client onboarding process by adding a vital prompt: Tell me how your parents and close family members handled finances growing up. How did you learn or not learn from them? How do you think that has manifested in your financial situation today?

In response, I received a treasure trove of hundreds of answers. Some were short and sweet, and others were as long as college essays. People painted their lives for me, rich in detail, scenarios, words, and moods, all of which ultimately formed the basis of the findings in this book. I saw that money wasn't actually the source of my clients' problems and that their habits and outcomes were symptoms of something else. There were underlying, deep-rooted issues that we had to resolve first before we could get anywhere with their finances.

From working with my clients, I identified three root causes that could explain the vast majority of problematic money behaviors in adulthood. There are infinite problems that lead to money trouble, but the reason I picked these three is because of how commonly they appear with my coaching clients and in national data. As I describe each root cause, I invite you to examine similarities between your habits and what you read. You may realize that you've experienced one or more of these root causes, which are not exclusive to one another. They describe a situation or set of situations that occur earlier in life and then heavily impact one's relationship to money later in life. To be sure, there are positive money root causes, which I will also describe. But since this book focuses on *changing* the habits of our childhoods, we will focus primarily on the root causes that result in problematic money behavior.

Feast and Famine

Maria, the single mother introduced in Chapter One, came from a family where money got spent, often in times of celebration, and when there was no money, they went into debt. They lived paycheck to paycheck. I call this root cause Feast and Famine, a play on the idiom "Feast or Famine." For these people, when things are going well, the celebration is grand and expensive; however, the financial lows are dark and feel like a raging money hangover. Maria, like many who have the Feast and Famine root cause, was following a similar behavior pattern as that of her parents. She certainly experienced a financial hangover when she finally added up all of her credit card debt.

Feast and Famine causes many adults to spend to the last cent. There is rarely a plan for money, and when things are not going well, there are constant worries over money and debt. Many people who experience Feast and Famine also came from childhoods where their parent(s) made a lower income. If you experienced Feast and Famine, it's common to have credit card debt, car loans and leases, personal lines of credit, and financial instability. Not only that, the debts seem to add on top of one another. Oftentimes people try to take out one debt to solve another, such as borrowing against their homes and moving debt around.[14]

People who have the Feast and Famine root cause tend to look for the next happiness hit, the next spending rush, to feel good. The moment they make money, they spend it, typically resulting in lavish Christmas gifts, glamorous vacations, and fancy meals to celebrate milestones. However, when the gravy runs dry, the pendulum swings in the other direction. Bills pile up and go unpaid. Nice purchases evolve into credit card debt. Car payments fall behind. The house may even wind up being seized by the bank. Then maybe the situation improves when the people with this root cause get more money again, and they can pay some of the bills. Like a temporary high, the good money never seems to last. Parents with the Feast and Famine root cause are too ashamed to tell their kids about this.

Feast and Famine issues lead to a lack of impulse control. With Feast and Famine, people do not think much beyond survival because they can only deal with what is most immediate. If you have this root cause, you're not alone. This root cause is the most common issue among those who have financial insecurity.

Adverse Events

Danielle came from a family that struggled with drug addiction. Her parents divorced when she was young. Her mother wasn't around much, but when she was, she'd take Danielle to drug dens. Danielle also spent much of her life trying to earn her father's love. Whenever she didn't meet his expectations, he would chastise her and tell her she would "grow up to be just like" her mom. He didn't adequately provide for Danielle either, leaving her from the age of nine to cook for herself, look after her brother, and clean the house. As a teenager, she fell in with the wrong crowd, became addicted to drugs, and even spent time in prison. Eventually, she was able to get the drug treatment she needed and married a kind husband, but many of her fears from childhood still linger.

Danielle felt an immense amount of shame, though she had been clean for fourteen years. She still had the desire to prove that she was worthy of her parents' approval, and carried guilt and struggled with her self-worth. As a result, Danielle often purchased things to make herself feel better: a Dooney & Burke bag, high-end cosmetics, clothing... Whenever she felt a moment of shame, she bought items that felt extravagant to her and put everything on credit cards, building up debt. Eventually, Danielle faced $80,000 of consumer debt, which took her six years to pay off. She had to downsize to an older home and used proceeds from her home sale to finish paying off her final debt, a car loan.

Then, Danielle's father was diagnosed with stage-four lung cancer. Danielle became an emotional wreck during her father's terminal illness and eventual passing. She felt that the only way she could be happy was to remodel her house until it was perfect. She took on $32,000 of debt to finish her home. When all was accounted for, Danielle felt even more shame and blamed herself as "irresponsible [for spending] all this money because my happiness depended on my outside circumstances."

If there's one issue I wish I could put all my energy into, it would be to rid the world of abusive relationships. In more than 96% of abusive relationships, abusers control their victims through money.[15] How might financial abuse appear? Typically, the victim isn't in control of their own money and has a meager amount to subsist on. Even if they make money, the abuser insists that the victim hand everything over to be managed by the abuser. The root cause of Danielle's money problem can be best categorized as Adverse Events, echoing the same categorization and findings by the ACEs study by CDC–Kaiser Permanente.

Within the Adverse Events root cause, parents or guardians often exert financial control over their children. Even if the situation is not deemed to be highly abusive, money and resources are used as a tool for controlling a child's behavior and making a parent's love conditional. Oftentimes, the parents may have a lack of understanding of child development or don't have adequate support to raise a child.[16] In other cases, the parents may have mental health or substance abuse problems or a record of being abused themselves when they were kids. They may also be struggling with life's pressures, such as a stressful job or financial insecurity. Perhaps most egregious of all, some parents simply do not care for their children.

Parents who have unrealistic expectations or put pressure on their child to succeed might withhold allowances and gifts until their child achieves a goal. In a situation where parents have more violent and unloving tendencies, they might withhold essential things, such as food or adequate heating. As a result, the key symptoms among children who experience Adverse Events is a lack of self-worth and the feeling that they will never be enough. Adverse Events may lead people to feel isolated and powerless for years, making it difficult to stand up for themselves. They often feel validated through external factors, like salaries, accolades, acceptances, appearances, and the opinion of others. No matter what they do, they seek approval—and self-validation does not count. Furthermore, those who have been raised in this kind of environment constantly search for emotional security but struggle to find it. Danielle admits, "If I looked a certain way and people noticed, then I would feel better about myself. And to be completely honest, I even wanted people to think I was someone important— like a celebrity!"

While children who experience Feast and Famine may have parents who exhibit unstable or unhealthy money behaviors, these parents aren't doing something intentional to harm or alter their children's innate need for love. However, in the Adverse Events root cause, the parent's behavior toward the child is harmful and warps the definition of love by making it conditional. For example, a parent in the Feast and Famine scenario might throw an extravagant birthday party because they love their child, though they can't figure out how to budget for it. An Adverse Events parent would provide a birthday party for their child only if their child met a set of unreasonable criteria.

From what I've observed among my clients, those who experienced Adverse Events exhibit adult financial behavior that is representative of *identity seeking*, meaning they are trying to ground their identity by chasing something that can define their self-worth. Dr. Jenny Wang, a clinical psychologist and author of *Permission to Come Home*, a book about how marginalized people can practice self-care, speaks of the disruption to one's sense of self. "When I think about trauma such as childhood abuse, a child's identity and relationship with the world get fragmented. They have an unstable sense of their self vs. others. They don't feel grounded or safe. When they look outside of themselves to find grounding... this leads to them chasing fame, substances, abusive relationships, material items... Pick your drug! They're chasing something that fills in the gap of a fractured identity that has not healed."

People who've experienced Adverse Events often strive for acknowledgment of their self-worth through achievement, looking for validation and input through awards, accolades, and career advancement. They might hold onto a large amount of savings, or they might spend all their money to pursue an identity expressed through materialism. Danielle's financial behavior represented identity-seeking through material items. Sadly, the moment that validation stops, it often leads to depression and self-harm. Dr. Wang further illustrates how lonely a childhood like Danielle's must have been. "When you come from a such a chaotic environment, you're seeking belonging, love, and affirmation from other folks. Growing up in a toxic environment alters and damages the child's identity. It impacts perception, how they react, how they show up in the world. They often seek ways where this affirmation can come quickly without recognizing how it could lead to negative outcomes like addiction."

The pain runs deep with Adverse Events. When I help these clients, I often strongly suggest that they also seek help from a licensed psychologist or psychiatrist. For some clients who have been told that they were worthless, they might find it pointless or difficult to take care of themselves as adults and don't treat their health as a priority. Budgeting and planning might get neglected, as these adults don't prioritize living for the future. For the other clients who chase achievement and status, they may appear to be high functioning from an outsider's perspective. For example, if you saw Danielle on the surface, she would be made up and wearing nice clothing; inside, however, she struggled with anxiety and self-doubt. It should be no surprise that people who have suffered severe Adverse Events have complex mental health challenges that need to be addressed and treated by professionals to bring their lives into moderation.

There is so much hope, though, if you've experienced Adverse Events. Even without a lot of psychological treatment, there are small and simple things you can do right now to help you feel better and start the journey of healing. I'll get into this more in Chapter Four, but just know that your life and money story can change if you're ready.

Scarce Immigrant

Esther was one of my friend-clients in the early days when I was looking for some feedback on my coaching techniques. She, like myself, came from an immigrant background, and we often bonded over our career paths. She and her husband appeared to travel and eat well and were the definition (at least to me) of up-and-coming, soon-to-be-rich people. But as we began to work together, one of the things that caught me completely by surprise was that Esther and her husband had more than $100,000 sitting in savings. They had no plans for it, and it was more than what they needed for an emergency fund. I asked what they were planning to do with it and noticed Esther had a hard time coming up with a response. She froze a lot in her decision-making. She beat herself up over spending money. She also had trouble communicating with her husband what the goal of all that money was.

Ultimately, I learned that this $100,000 was their security blanket. Growing up, Esther saw how much her immigrant parents had to scrimp and save. When she wanted to buy something, her parents would tell her to "wait until it was discounted, and discounted, and discounted again, until it was final discount.... My parents were very scarce with every penny, and in the beginning years, I knew that their income was not great." Esther saw money as freedom. In her early adulthood, she also experienced a season of unstable employment, and a large savings account helped assuage her fears regarding her career. Thus whenever I asked Esther about taking on more risk, she wanted to back out.

Many of the people I coach are immigrants or children of immigrants. I'm an immigrant too. Most immigrants in the US are not people with much privilege, and many immigrant children saw their parents struggle to make it in a foreign country, where their tongues got twisted as they learned new languages and their faces flushed with embarrassment if they committed a cultural faux pas. Frugality is very common. It is not unusual for immigrant parents to save for everything, work long hours, and place a strong emphasis on education for their children to build a better life. Money is limited and often split between the family in the US and a larger family to support back in their country of origin, who often come first. I call this root cause the Scarce Immigrant.

Even though I use the word "scarce," frugality is not the key resulting money behavior. I have met many children of immigrants who are frugal by imitating their parents and then go on to invest their savings. They may even reach FIRE at a similar pace as I did. That's healthy! Instead, Scarce Immigrant leads to a money problem where one is risk-avoidant. People with the Scarce Immigrant root cause often come from a background where they or their families fled violent and oppressive regimes or countries where there was active warfare. They were scared for their lives, not knowing who was monitoring their every move or trying to throw them in jail or attack them physically. I remember my parents used to remind me weekly of how hard things were back in China. They wanted to leave behind poverty and malnutrition. They didn't want to be thrown into jail on false charges. They grew up with cautionary whispers of *Don't stand out in the wrong way. Don't get into trouble. You can get killed for misbehaving.* They learned to pick safe jobs that a society will always need. Play it safe, always. Stay alive. Keep your kids alive. Even though the Cultural Revolution ended, staying in the People's Republic of China didn't feel like it could lead to a prosperous future for my family. My parents took the most considerable risk of their lives by leaving everything they knew behind. These immigrants learn not to break too many rules or take side steps as adults. I have often found that Scarce Immigrant parents love their children so fiercely that they try to protect their children from any harm. That is where their fears come from—love.

Professor Zane at UC Davis adds another nuance regarding the pressures of expectations on immigrant parents. He says that immigrant parents are conservative with money because "many immigrant parents want to build wealth but don't know whom to trust. They often go into business with their families and relatives, people from their culture. There is a huge cultural expectation not to bring shame upon your family by losing money. That is why you also see a lot of investments in homes, because it's physical. They can see it. They can't see the stock market. Immigrants need to have more tangible kinds of proof about their wealth."

Immigrant parents are most likely to stockpile their money instead of investing it, and favor real estate over the stock market. Many immigrants fled countries where the banking system was not as stable, where they might've seen governments seize assets at a whim and suffered uncontrolled inflation. Homeownership is often regarded as the pinnacle of financial success because you can always physically touch your home and call it yours.

As a result, those who have the Scarce Immigrant root cause often follow the safe path. Most commonly, I find that they take longer to get into investing or side-hustling and sit on large piles of cash to have a sense of comfort. The key to accounting for this root cause in personal finance is getting more comfortable with doing things while scared. To this, I say do it scared, but do it anyway.

Other Root Causes Around Money

What if you've never experienced any of the above root causes? Maybe your childhood was relatively uneventful. You might have experienced some root causes that led to bad money management, but your behavior around money might not be as extreme as the examples presented. Possibly, you might not have yet experienced so much stress that you go into survival mode (not that I'm wishing such an event on you), so life is pretty stable for you right now. That's great, because that means that you can benefit from the teachings of this book without having to fight a difficult battle, like an episode of depression or loss of income. In the sections in the book where I provide advice by root cause, you can feel free to skip some of the applications and look for the more generalized advice that I provide to everyone. You can also peruse the advice anyway and adopt what speaks to you.

Or maybe you have experienced some of the root causes, but you've done the very hard work of healing your inner child, whether that's through therapy, life coaching, or some other kind of work. Just as there are people who follow their parents' examples, Dr. Wang says many children end up doing the opposite of what their parents did. "Let's say that you grew up seeing Mom and Dad abuse alcohol. Some people see that as being very negative, and as adults, they do everything they can to avoid drinking." When it comes to money, your adult behavior around money may actually be stable and rational then, because you saw how your parents' bad habits led to financial instability. Hence, your ability to cope with pressure has matured, and you are set up for future wealth.

Another reason the three root causes above might not apply to you is that your childhood may have been very positive, and those habits and behaviors that defined your childhood led to positive outcomes. Though I devote the majority of my book discussing the implications of having experienced a negative root cause, I also want to acknowledge that positive ones exist and they can often lead to positive money outcomes:

- You grew up with parents with higher-than-average socioeconomic status. This is the opposite of the Feast and Famine root cause, where most parents are low-income earners. If one's parents are wealthy (in terms of both income and net worth), children in these households never have to worry about hunger, shelter, healthcare, and education, allowing them more room to dream and take bigger risks. There is a lot of power in growing up in a privileged environment.

- You grew up with few adverse events in your childhood. If you experienced fewer of the adverse events cited in Chapter Two and in the description of Adverse Events above, you are more likely to have good mental health as an adult and less likely to spin out of control during a stressful situation.

- Your parents openly discussd money, usually with a neutral-to-positive outlook. You may have even had an allowance growing up and learned budgeting as part of your financial education.

- You were taught at a young age to avoid debt, either by your parents and guardians or through a class. When I was in college, the local credit union offered a class on credit to anyone who was on the leadership board of a student group. That course taught me a lot about avoiding credit advances and carrying a credit card balance, going more in depth than my parents ever did about revolving credit.

- When your parents made an important decision, they did so by relying on facts and analysis. Data-driven decision-making is an example of executive function, and the more one does this, the better one gets at making these decisions.

Regardless of whether you saw yourself represented by a root cause, I encourage you to consider the solutions and advice in the rest of the book and take what speaks to you.

Trigger, Action, Reward: The Spending Cycle

The impacts of the three root causes I described are generational. We have to break cycles so history will not repeat itself. Can we pause for a moment and acknowledge that this is actually... really exciting? That from negative, depressive, heartbreaking situations, anyone reading this book can make an immediate change in their mindset using this one technique that I'm going to teach you? It doesn't require any fancy degrees, and it comes at little to no cost to you. All the solution asks for is that be open to changing your habits. If you don't feel ready yet, that's okay; I still encourage you to check out my solution. This book will be here for you when you are ready.

Habits are mental shortcuts our brains take to spend less energy making decisions. Sometimes these practices are fantastic; if we learn to do something well over time, it gets easier and we get better. If a habit is incorrect, however, acting on it can worsen life situations. In Charles Duhigg's book *The Power of Habit*, he asks the reader to think of what we do first when we wake up in the morning. Is it hopping in the shower? Checking our email? Grabbing a doughnut from the kitchen counter? It takes a second for us to think and tell someone else what we do every day, but when we wake up, we don't think about it. We just do it. That's the automation that is happening in our brain, and it would make sense that this happens a lot in the morning because we're still foggy from our sleep!

How do habits happen? They are usually triggered by a strong idea, sensation, or situation that activates our brain. In the morning, the trigger is usually our alarm or simply jolting awake. Once our brains light up, we draw upon our memories from when our habits first formed (such as in our childhood) to decide on the next step. Consider hunger: When we are triggered by a hunger sensation in our stomach, our bodies direct us to find food. A very strong situational trigger might be the death of a loved one, which impacts our brains so much that we almost can't function. I have often had to wait for months to hear back from clients who are grieving. Here are some examples of the most common emotional and situational triggers I've observed in coaching:

Emotional triggers: Hunger, anger, anxiety, loneliness, tiredness, stress, sadness.

Situational triggers: An accidental/unexpected health event; a new household member to care for (a new child, an elderly parent); grief over separation/loss (the death of a loved one, divorce, geographical relocation); a stressful job/toxic workplace; and recent mental illness or worsening of mental illness symptoms.

As humans, we have all experienced one or more of these triggers. They create real needs that we have to address. To meet the trigger, we take an *action*, and as a result of the action our brains feel a *reward* that meets the need in the moment. Here are two examples of the spending cycle:

Trigger: Hunger. You are hungry and don't feel like cooking.

Action: You hit the Order button on a delivery app to satiate your hunger.

Reward: The food is delivered. You eat, and your hunger is satisfied.

Here's another example of a spending cycle that was very common for me:

Trigger: Stress. I need an item shipped quickly.

Action: I buy it on Amazon without doing any research elsewhere.

Reward: I get the item delivered quickly.

When it comes to spending, Feast and Famine leads to impulsive spending, usually on a consumer good or an experience. If you have experienced Adverse Events, you might find yourself feeling worthless, so you spend in a way to get love externally (one such example might be cosmetic surgery, so you feel you look better). The Scarce Immigrant root cause leads you to avoid risk, so you might further hoard your money to feel safe. The issue with all these actions is that they are just temporary Band-Aids addressing the *symptoms*, not the underlying problems that are causing the triggers. Then as we struggle with money over time, we begin to think that we are bad at managing money. In addition, we might not actually be aware that we're doing these actions out of habit! I have heard from many people that they have no idea how they racked up so much debt; they don't realize the debt comes from hundreds, if not thousands, of habitual purchases over time.

At some point in our childhood, we probably experienced a temporary solution to our needs. We saw a reward that worked at the moment. And our limbic system tells us that if it worked historically, as it did when we were children, it should work again in our adult lives! If our mental health is not great, we also don't want to overthink things. Our brains are already overstimulated, so we rely on our habits and instincts to get by. If we saw our parents engage in shopping to feel better, then we, too, might shop. If we saw our parents drink alcohol when under stress, then we are also more likely to drink to cope with pressure. An incorrect or scarce Trigger, Action, Reward

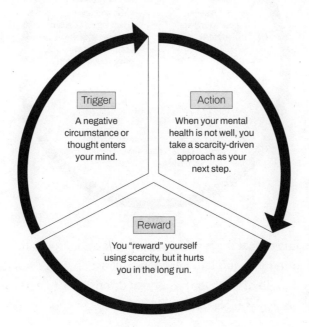

habit cycle might form when our mental health is not optimal, and while this cycle typically leads to a short-term satiation of our psychological need, it is not a long-term solution.

Over time, these habit loops become a cycle, which I call the *spending cycle*. It repeats itself and is self-perpetuating. When we act on scarcity, we are just trying to survive, not thrive; we don't actually receive the proper reward that allows us to heal from a trigger, and that is due to our taking the incorrect action. Thus, the next time we feel the trigger, we repeat the same action, leading to the same short-term reward, yet this does not solve the underlying problem. I saw many people—including myself—pedal through this cycle endlessly. It was because of this cycle that I felt lacking on a frugal budget when I was trying to save money living in New York City.

The Solution: Change the Action

Trigger
A negative circumstance or thought enters your mind.

Action
You address the underlying root cause and also take a low cost approach to solve your problem.

Reward
You heal from your wounds, and the impact of the trigger on your mental health lessens over time.

Now that we know what triggers our spending, we can fix it with just one thing: Aim for a long-term reward through a different action. This change in behavior is often the opposite of what you have been doing. It has to address the underlying root cause, why you got triggered in the first place! You have a valid reason for getting emotional; your heart wants something. Your heart's desires are valid and should not be ignored! If you patch it over with a temporary solution, you'll keep cycling. That's why you have to dig deep and make sure that your action is directly meeting your psychological needs, and not just a surface-level patch. Furthermore, your new action should also ideally be low-cost. Most people going through a spending cycle are squandering money they don't have. Thus, we want the action to address your true issue and be cost-effective so that you don't spend yourself into debt.

All you have to do is act differently to change your life. It sounds straightforward, but it's hard because I'm asking you to change your life, one tiny action at a time, which could feel in some ways counterintuitive and maybe uncomfortable. However, I promise that you will likely save money and get wealthier over time if you stick with this. The changes we make to your spending cycle will solve your ultimate issues so that you'll find yourself entering unhealthy spending cycles less frequently over time. What might these cycles look like based on the root cause?

Feast and Famine

Maria's money issues stemmed from her having grown up with Feast and Famine as her root cause. Her family liked to splurge on experiences and made a big show that this is what a good family does. Whenever Maria faced conflict, which was often over how she parented her daughter, she was then triggered to spend because she wanted to prove to her family that she was a great mom. She impulsively purchased things to feel better. Internally, however, she was struggling to clear her loans and make a path toward retirement. Here is Maria's spending cycle.

In Maria's case, she needed a new action that proved she was a good mother without spending a lot of money. She needed to pivot toward a low-spend activity that still allowed her to enjoy quality time with her daughter. It could be as simple as going with her daughter to a park, sharing a quiet meal at home, or just being present for her daughter. Over time, she would get the desired outcome of having closeness with her daughter while achieving the monetary result of saving more money.

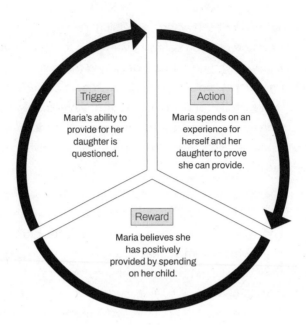

A new spending cycle helped Maria change her habits and gain insight into herself. Once she recognized how much of her impulse spending was tied to how she viewed herself as a mother, she learned to regulate those thoughts. Part of the reason why she moved out of her parents' home was because much of the criticism came directly from her family. Now ensconced in an adorable little in-law unit on her landlord's property, she found her mind clearing.

In the tranquility of the bright rental, Maria didn't hear criticisms in her head. She didn't feel like she had to always be "on" to present the best version of herself to her family. If she got clothes for her daughter via hand-me-downs from another local mother, her family would never know. One of the keys to Maria's success was that she reduced the source of her triggers. In the beginning of applying this solution, she wrote me, "I am finding so much more joy now in little things. Yesterday I was hungry while out. Normally I would get fast food, but I stopped myself and figured I could spend that $13 and buy some cereal and milk, which I needed anyway. I had cereal for dinner. I never would have done that before." Maria was able to give her brain enough space to plan for ideas that she could execute when triggers appeared. In other words, she could think ahead and reason with her impulsive side!

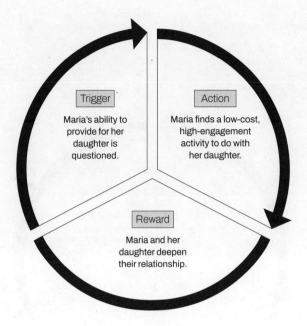

Adverse Event

Danielle felt stuck in a cycle when she was accumulating her consumer debt. She mentioned to me, "It's really hard to let go of thought patterns you've had your whole life. It's hard living day to day and be like, no, I'm not my past. I cannot seem to get a good financial plan in place. I get depressed when I feel like I'm not making progress. Then I spend so that I feel like there is physical evidence that I can be successful." She wanted everything to be perfect on the outside because that's how she thought she could reach peace on the inside.

Danielle's triggers were most often feeling shame, anxiety, or stress over what other people thought of her because she defined her self-worth using other people's opinions—especially those of her parents, who have both since passed away. Danielle's temporary reward was the dopamine hit she received from purchasing things and taking care of her family, which made her feel like she was a good caretaker and doing something valuable with her life.

However, this didn't solve her long-term problem: that she has yet to practice self-love. To do that, she had to stop caring about what other people think of her and focus on herself. Danielle needed a new spending cycle where the ultimate reward would be to love herself, and she needed to acknowledge that somehow in an action. A new spending cycle for Danielle is one where she starts moving away from her past demons to create a more beautiful, loving future.

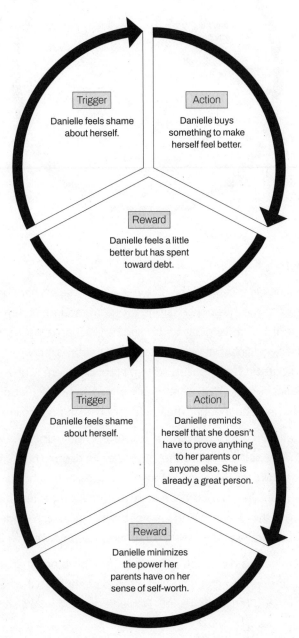

Trigger
Danielle feels shame about herself.

Action
Danielle buys something to make herself feel better.

Reward
Danielle feels a little better but has spent toward debt.

Trigger
Danielle feels shame about herself.

Action
Danielle reminds herself that she doesn't have to prove anything to her parents or anyone else. She is already a great person.

Reward
Danielle minimizes the power her parents have on her sense of self-worth.

Danielle has since become much kinder to herself. One of the greatest pleasures I had from coaching her was seeing her slowly heal from her past and view herself as successful without relying on the opinions of her family members. I often had to remind her that her parents were no longer here and couldn't criticize her from beyond the grave, something that felt very new to her. She told me, "I'm still learning that I'd been triggered by my parents. I'm seeing that they failed me, and that I shouldn't have had to grow up like that. God has brought me so far, and people who've heard my testimony cannot believe that I'm telling the truth. God turns our lives around. And people deserve another chance. It's not too late. Just do it scared, and if you mess up, keep going."

Scarce Immigrant

Esther's trigger when it came to stockpiling money was uncertainty. When she saw the volatility of stocks, it triggered her anxiety. Then, to soothe her anxiety, she sought two actions to help her feel secure: save up cash, or spend on creature comforts, like eating out and traveling. Esther's reward was knowing she did something financially safe. Still, there was a little bird whispering in her ear (me, as her friend and coach) that maybe her security blanket could downsize to a handkerchief instead.

It took some time for Esther to recognize that investing did not have to be scary (more about this in Chapter Eight). My recommendation to her was to lean into the discomfort of her uncertainty and use those triggering thoughts to nudge her toward investing. For every time that she felt uncertainty, she would then stop and rethink, and see that investing would be her path toward financial freedom and security.

Esther has embraced investing over time. She shared, "I realized I needed to make money long-term . . . I used to think if you just knew enough, you could also find a way to outsmart the market by timing it and buying stocks. Investing brings a lot of fear. Just seeing the ups and downs, the volatility." In working with me, Esther realized that she had a lot of mental blocks around change and transition, and she turned to therapy to help her through her anxieties, as "being more mentally stable helped with not having to reach out for these dopamine hits like my eating out." Eventually, Esther has become comfortable

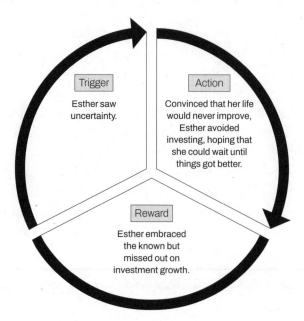

with embracing all aspects of investing, including managing her own 401(k), IRA, and taxable brokerage accounts! She has confidently stepped into the brilliant role of being her own portfolio investing manager and finally understands that a healthy amount of risk in her life is worth undertaking.

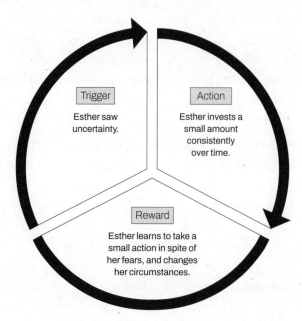

Now It's Your Turn

How might you apply the spending cycle to your own life? First, wait until you are feeling calm and neutral and have a good hour to sit down and do some journaling. Then, I want you to work on identifying your existing spending cycles and brainstorm how they can be changed. To do so, I encourage you to remember the last three to five times you impulsively spent money or felt paralyzing fear and anxiety around money. Observe whether these moments had common emotions or circumstances surrounding them. Let's write them down.

My triggering emotions:

My triggering circumstances:

Based on the above, write a Trigger, Action, Reward spending cycle for yourself that summarizes how you spend money. Describe in a few words, as I did in the examples, how you get triggered, what you end up doing, and what you feel as a reward in the moment.

My Trigger:

My Action:

My Reward:

Now comes the change—making your new spending cycle! Using some of the examples described above to brainstorm new ideas, think hard about the psychological need you would like to address with your spending cycle. What emotions are you trying to meet? What circumstances do you want to escape? This is the root of your spending. Now imagine what life would be like with these needs met. Imagine having the freedom not to be affected by these emotions over time. The reality is that your triggers will never go away, but with mindset work and change, your emotional response to them will become less volatile.

Here are some examples that I have personally experienced or seen happen among my coaching clients.

Trigger	Old action	New action	New reward
Loneliness	Eat out with a friend	Invite a friend over for dessert	You have companionship at a lower cost than a restaurant meal.
Boredom	Shop online	Join a meetup group	You have something enjoyable to do.
Grief due to losing someone you love	Turn to retail therapy to help you cope	Turn to talk therapy to help you process grief	You receive true and tested coping mechanisms to live with your grief.
Stress from work	Book an expensive vacation	Take a staycation to rest	You get the rest that you need at a very low cost.
Fear about becoming a first-time parent	Spend money on child-related items to try to be the perfect parent	Deprioritize things in your life so you can focus on being a new parent	You put less pressure on yourself to be a perfect parent while focusing on what is important for your child.
Defeat and frustration after making a mistake	Buy something that makes you feel better	Affirm yourself positively, then see what you can do to avoid repeating the mistake	You work on self-improvement and do not depend on a purchase to feel affirmed.

Remember, you are changing your action to directly meet what your heart truly desires while also saving money. If you follow the old actions above, you are likely to feel better for a bit, but mostly at the expense of spending money impulsively to do so. I always think back to how I used to take vacations from my stressful management consulting job, when in reality I just wanted to sleep at home. Many of my vacations in my early twenties were a huge strain on my budget, and I also didn't sleep as much as I wanted because I wanted to experience everything. While the vacations were fun, they didn't really make me feel rested. In many of the new actions in the examples above, you are still doing something, but at a lower cost than the old action, and addressing the root cause of your issue. Win, win, win!

Your new Trigger, Action, Reward cycle should look different from your old one. It should feel more hopeful, optimistic, and loving. It usually involves spending less money without thought. Write out your new cycle, then try it out over the next week and see how you feel.

My Trigger:

My Action:

My Reward:

I hope seeing these examples makes you feel less alone in your money journey. You are part of a community of people worldwide who have experienced something similar to your life and have acted similarly. Thankfully, this community is going to grow and prosper. All these people whose root causes may have led to less-than-ideal money habits can move forward and thrive and grow wealthy.

CHAPTER FOUR

YOUR ONE NEXT STEP

If you focus on one thing for a short amount of time, you are likely to get it done. Then you get excited! Little endorphins race through your body as you feel a sense of accomplishment. We need that feeling. Nothing is more motivating than a jolt of energy from feeling capable. As you read this book, I want you to set one goal—your One Next Step.

Becoming Fit Because I Didn't Want to Die

It was not until age thirty-eight that I began exercising regularly, going to the gym three times a week or hitting the mat in my living room. I finally had a big enough health scare that motivated me to commit to my fitness. My follow-through was less morbid: I just realized I had been setting the wrong goals for many years.

As a child, I thought I was bad at physical activity. I received the equivalent of a D for gymnastics in elementary school in the Netherlands, and this trend continued for years. I would later learn that Dutch gymnastics was not like an average American gym class, as it included tumbling, jumping over vaults, and walking on balance beams. I also never saw my parents work out until I was in high school. They weren't into sports; my father was a brainiac academic, and my mother preferred spending her free time watching cooking shows.

As an adult, I had to restart my fitness journey several times. I knew intellectually that there may be severe health consequences if I didn't take care of my physical health. I was one of those people who began gym memberships in January and never went back. Every attempt ended up with me reverting back to not exercising. I often used being busy as an excuse, and then I would feel there was no point to working out because I didn't see muscle tone within a month.

Finally, in 2023, I was able to stick to an exercise routine soon after the birth of my second child around Christmas the previous year. I'd gone through a lung-related issue that landed me in the ICU. When I got out, I realized that if I put no effort into my body, then each future health scare might be my last; but if I worked out, then at least I could increase my chances of living. So other than the existential threat of possibly dying, what else changed?

My goal setting.

Prior to 2023, I was under the impression that I had to devote thirty minutes to working out each time. That made it hard for me because there were days when that time was very precious. With a newborn whom my husband could mind for only about half an hour before I needed to breastfeed, I decided to change the expectation to just fifteen minutes of exercise. I also hated running and yoga, so in 2023 I told myself that I could do any fitness I wanted. (I gravitated toward weightlifting.) I celebrated each time I went, sometimes with a small video of my workout or a flexing selfie that I posted to social media afterward. I also learned that six packs are really hard to develop and that I shouldn't expect muscles to pop up suddenly.

It took years, but my fourth attempt at working out was the huge unlock I needed to commit to the most unattainable habit in my life. Let's use some of the lessons I learned from my fitness journey to help you commit to your personal finance goals.

Regret Is an Unproductive Emotion

Probably every person I have ever taught or coached has told me that they wished they had started caring earlier about their personal finances, and this includes people in their twenties all the way up to their sixties. They think it's too late now to start, just like I thought that starting my exercise journey at age thirty-eight seemed quite late.

But regret is a highly unproductive emotion. Whenever we feel it, we put ourselves back into a scarcity mindset. We sit in the past. We beat ourselves up for the things we did insufficiently and revisit some of the most shameful, painful, vulnerable memories of our childhood. We don't feel good when we live in regret! The sad truth is that we can't change the past. So, one essential thing I hope you take away from this book is that if you are feeling regret, put a timer on it.

For example, on the first day of your commitment, pay attention to the moment you feel regret and set a timer on your watch or phone alarm for two hours. During those two hours, you are welcome to let the thoughts and feelings sit in your mind. It's important to engage with our emotional selves. By the end of the two hours, make a conscious decision to stop lingering on those feelings. You can take a few big, deep breaths. Consider walking around your building or neighborhood to get some fresh air, as oxygen does wonders for our brain function. Perhaps start a different activity that requires all of your concentration. Your goal is to exit the regret spiral by the end of the two hours.

The next day that you feel regret, set the timer for one hour and forty-five minutes. The day after that, lower the timer by another fifteen minutes. Do this until you are able to exit your regret spiral within fifteen minutes or less.

Also, remember you have access to all the knowledge in the world. You can search online via your phone, hire people for professional help, and learn from those who have done what you would like to do. We will compare against only ourselves and focus on progress over perfection, commitment over achievement. The best entrepreneurs in the world are not necessarily the most intelligent, beautiful, or talented. They often have innate talent, but when talent meets hard work, hard work with talent beats raw talent any time.

Goal-setting Rules

I know a thing or two about setting goals. Many of the most difficult things I've accomplished in my life were the result of breaking down a big ambition into smaller, more achievable steps, which I then implemented and problem-solved, to work my way to the bigger goal. Knowing how to set realistic markers can be the difference between achieving and giving up. Here are three rules that I recommend you consider as you set your next financial goal.

90% Rule

Your goals might be incredibly worthy but also hard to achieve. People don't just pay off $100,000 in student loans overnight or immediately save up a quarter-million-dollar down payment to purchase a home. It's easy to give up in the short term, just like I did with exercising when I saw no muscle development a month after working out. I call my first rule of goal setting the 90% Rule: Your first goal should be a goal that you believe with 90% certainty that you can achieve. Not 100%; if you were completely certain you could do it, then you'd have done it by now. I'm not saying this to disparage whether you've achieved a goal, but rather trying to communicate the level of difficulty we are aiming for. To set yourself up for success, create an objective that feels aspirational but also achievable. If you don't reach your first financial aim, then you are likely to give up and not want to continue. You would feel frustrated, and I want to prevent that.

For example, if you have never put any time or thought toward personal finances, guess what? By reading this book, you are doing it now! How much time do you think you can commit to learning or doing something about your personal finances going forward? How much time this week are you using to read this book? Start with that! I suggest the ideal amount of time to doing your finances is one hour a week. However, that might not be feasible for you; but does half an hour a week feel about 90% doable to you? Then let's start with that. Ignore what I say about the "ideal time" and set an amount of time that works for you. You hurt yourself by setting unrealistic goals, and realistic targets should feel easy and make you feel good as you start your journey.

Input, Not Output

If you follow the suggestions in this book in the order in which I wrote the chapters, then you are more likely than not to achieve financial freedom and build wealth. That is fantastic news! But life can sometimes get in the way. Health, external political upheaval, accidents, economic crises, and lawsuits are just the tip of the randomness that can affect us. These setbacks can move your financial progress back by months, even years. Because of this, I don't focus on people achieving a specific net worth number or month to get debt-free. You're tying yourself to a number, just like I was doing when trying to get on some magazine list for entrepreneurs. This type of output goal is not productive and does not account for the randomness of life. Instead, I suggest you focus on inputs.

Inputs in finance are things like time spent on personal finance, the amount you can send to a debt, savings, or investing account, the number of times you commit to getting therapy, the number of books you read about personal finance, the number of times you completely log all your expenses in the past week, how many job applications you send out per day, and the number of networking calls you make. Notice how specific these inputs are; they are about holding you accountable for the effort you put in, instead of the result you get out.

Time-bound

It is also essential to time-bound your goal, meaning you create a deadline for yourself. I don't mean a deadline like, "I will be a millionaire by age thirty." Time-bounding is more that you need to build a habit over time and be consistent with this habit. It's like when I decided to commit to going to the gym three times a week for at least two months.

Hot tip: This deadline is not the be-all and end-all, and you can change it as you pursue this goal. However, I like providing a deadline because when you achieve it, you can celebrate it. It goes back to the critical mind work—you need to feel good about your efforts and have a sense of accomplishment. To start, set your very first goal to take about one to two months to complete. One to two months is just enough time for the goal to be meaningful and for a habit to start to set in.

Sample Beginner Goals

You can do great things, but those things build up from little things. In this section, I provide some sample beginner goals, and while they are specific to each root cause, you can really pick any one of them and be well on your way toward abundance. Feel free to copy the exact goal or modify it to fit your unique personality and situation. This will be what you will commit to as your One Next Step after you finish this book.

	Everyone	Feast and Famine	Adverse Events	Scarce Immigrant
Sample Goal One	Devote one hour a week to financial planning	Pause for twenty-four hours on purchasing	Use a gratitude journal every day	Have one networking conversation each week
Sample Goal Two	Aim to save at least $___ a month	Set up automated savings transfers	Practice self-affirmation every day	Invest $___ you don't mind losing

Goals for Everyone

If personal finance is a new skill for you, you need to devote time to it. When you first learned math in school, you had a specific period in your school schedule devoted to math class so you could learn concepts from a teacher and reinforce the knowledge with homework. Similarly, you will need to dedicate time for personal finance as an adult.

Money Happy Hour. If you work forty-hour weeks, chances are you work around two thousand hours a year. How many hours do you devote to tracking the money you make and growing it? If you put full-time work hours and effort into your finances, the finances can improve. However, it's not realistic for most of us to do that. Instead, I have found that dedicating even just one hour a week is a great start and helps you reset your financial life. I call this the Money Happy Hour (or Sexy Monday Date, for those who are married or in a relationship where you share finances). Use this time however you wish, whether that's tracking your expenses, running a money errand, self-educating and reading books like this one, or chatting with your partner to align on money goals.

Monthly savings amount: One of the most commonly asked questions in personal finance is, How much am I supposed to save? The keyword in this question is "supposed." Personal finance is personal, so there is no perfect amount of savings. However, we do get one benefit in personal finance: Math does not lie. The earlier you get into the habit of saving and investing, the more you save and invest and the faster you get to financial freedom. It's that simple. So, think back to the 90% Rule. What number can you realistically save (or use to pay extra toward a debt) in a month? Don't overthink it—just start with a number. In the next few months, aim to pay yourself first by sending that amount to a savings account or debt, then live off the remainder. (We'll go into more detail in Chapters Five and Eight, focused on debt and budgeting, to give you more guidance on how to do this.)

Goals for Feast and Famine

For money behaviors that are the result of Feast and Famine, we want to move away from short-term planning and make saving money easy. Both the twenty-four-hour pause and automatic monthly savings are ways that take away the ability for your impulsive brain to be the main decision maker when it comes to spending. It's kind of like putting your reptilian brain on ice.

Twenty-four-hour pause: Whenever you find yourself ready to make an impulse purchase, wait twenty-four hours before doing anything. This pause forces you to consider the purchase and ask yourself if you genuinely need it. It allows the impulsive part of our brain to rest and for us to engage the cortex part of our brain, which takes time to work. Many people have found this technique very easy to implement and successfully cut down on a lot of their impulse shopping. I used this very technique myself in high school after I saw a friend of mine put clothing she liked "on hold" with the cashier (not something that can be commonly done now) for twenty-four hours so she could decide on it later.

Automatic monthly savings: Too many financial habits have become automated over time. How do we change them? Automation is, in and of itself, an electronic habit that you don't always notice once it's been set up, but it can be the antidote to your impulsive habits. One of my favorite ways to automate in finances is to create automated savings or transfers. If you have never saved before, I recommend your One Next Step to be setting up an online high-yield savings account (refer to page 210 of the appendix) and creating a monthly automatic transfer from your checking account, ideally on the days you get paid. If you ever need the money, you can always access the savings account and transfer the funds back to your checking account.

Goals for Adverse Events

For those who've experienced Adverse Events, your first goals should focus on self-love. We have to heal your childhood wounds and move your brain away from the poisonous thoughts of your past.

Daily gratitude journal: Consider writing in a gratitude journal at the end of each day, documenting at least one thing to be grateful for. Suppose you are a perfectionist or people pleaser. In that case, you may often focus on what did not go well, which makes it more difficult to appreciate what you have. This activity is a very doable and rewarding exercise that helps us end each day positively. It is also a beautiful collection of writing that you can look back on after a few months' time to see how much you can be grateful for.

Loving words: Affirm yourself with loving words at least once daily. Do you like love letters? Do you get them a lot? Consider this beginner goal if you answered yes then no to these questions. A fundamental reason why we often feel pressure to please others or live up to others' opinions of ourselves is because we don't spend enough time loving ourselves and affirming the uniqueness that we each possess. I love affirmation exercises (perfect when I'm brushing my teeth!) because they provide a quick and much-needed mood booster without needing to spend money or wait for someone else's approval.

Goals for Scarce Immigrant

Those of you with the Scarce Immigrant root cause want to avoid risk, so my sample goal for your One Next Step is to start engaging with risk a bit more. Doing a little bit at a time will make you feel more comfortable stepping out and doing things scared, in life and in money.

Weekly networking: Networking is important to build your network to improve your skills, broaden your career prospects, increase your earning potential, and so much more! Immigrants in particular are vulnerable to feeling alone in the workforce by sheer fact that they are in the minority, so they don't have the advantage of the majority. I credit every success I have encountered in my career to networking. I know that on merit alone, I might not succeed. (I'll go into more detail later in Chapter Seven.) I encourage you to try to work up to having at least one networking conversation a week, even if you're not currently looking for a job change.

Invest an amount you don't mind losing: You're probably terrified of the idea of investing because you're scared that you might lose money. As the adage goes, There is no risk without reward. I want you to try investing right now, even if you don't feel ready, because the truth is, no one is truly ever ready. Set aside an amount of money you don't mind losing and put it toward investments. Want a greater challenge? Do this every month so that you become more used to the idea of seeing yourself as an investor.

I was filming some of my workouts and saw one day I didn't want to work out. I procrastinated, checked my email and social media, and did anything but move my arms with weights. I even began making up different movements toward the end that had little effect on my workout goals. That was one of those workout days that *barely* counted... and that's okay! Not every attempt will look the same when you start on your One Next Step. Sometimes you will do it well, and other times you will miss the goal completely. I want you to have fun, love yourself, and embrace this positively. Don't beat yourself up whenever you fall short of the goal. If you are consistently missing your target, make it easier. This simply means that you are aligning it more toward your real life. Remember, it's not how you start; it's how you finish.

CHAPTER FIVE

DEBT

In 1994, Dave Ramsey published the book *Total Money Makeover*, which took the personal finance world by storm. Ramsey understood that money is emotional and people are impatient, and it benefited people to pay off the smallest debt balance first and then move to the next smallest. This way of paying off debt, called the Snowball Method, was pretty groundbreaking. However, the tone used in the book and the company that he built to help others become debt-free were based in fear and shame. *Debt is bad. Having any debt means there is something wrong and you have to fix it.* He reminds me of the brim-and-firestone preaching that particular churches like to use, just about finance.

I'm delighted that the new generation of personal finance writers is kinder when discussing debt. Dave Ramsey has undoubtedly impacted millions of American households and helped many people get out of debt, but today, it's clear that shame-based coaching can harm our mental health. As a mental health–focused finance coach, I favor a gentler style. Everyone is worthy of love, and self-love can inspire one to transform.

Your Debt Does Not Define You

Let's make this abundantly clear. Someone who has debt is not a bad person. It does not mean you have some fundamental character flaw or did something immoral. Debt accumulation could have resulted from your upbringing, how your parents and close family handled it, or how the community around you regarded money.

I have had many clients who had debt that resulted from situations or circumstances beyond their control. These situations include a sudden loss of income that emergency savings can't cover, unexpected medical bills, a lack of funds to pursue higher education, and unprofitable business investments. I'll share a few examples to show how people who appear to be well off and comfortable can still very quickly rack up tens or hundreds of thousands of dollars in debt without any indication that they made a mistake to begin with. I've seen all of the below in coaching.

Expensive divorces: According to Nolo, the average cost of divorce in 2019 ranged from $4,100 (when there are no disputes) to over $20,000 (when proceedings go to trial).[17] In most marriages, one spouse often makes more than the other. On average, men earn more than women, and women tend to be awarded child custody 80% of the time.[18] So, what happens after a man and a woman divorce? The woman is left with a hefty legal bill, lower income than the man, and a greater share of child-rearing costs, all while having to go to work most of their waking hours. An impossible situation to stay out of debt, if you ask me. Most child-support payments are also inadequate. The single mother with majority custody of the child has to rent or own a larger home than the single dad. She also has to lower her expenses (versus when she was sharing finances with her ex-husband) to adjust to her lower income. This is a setup for failure. I have coached several single mothers who struggled to make ends meet.

Student loans: According to the US Federal Reserve, one in seven Americans—or forty-five million people—have student debt totaling $1.6 trillion.[19] There are two dynamics at play when it comes to student debt among the people I have coached.

First, most jobs require undergraduate degrees, so anyone who graduates with a college degree should see some return on their investment in their education. However, not all jobs that require graduate degrees pay a high enough income for that achievement to be worth it. For example, a one-year master's program in teaching costs on average over $19,000.[20] However, in a national database of teachers' salaries, the average first-year differential in compensation is about $2,760.[21] It could take years before wage increases pay back the degree. This was the case with Wendy, whom you met in Chapter One. The value of her original loans was significantly less than what she owed years later after she started working because her income unfortunately did not increase significantly to help her pay off the loans.

The second dynamic is that highly paid jobs, like in the medical, legal, and business fields, require you to spend years in school. Most medical schools require four years of coursework and then a residency. Take Harvard Medical School as an example: One could incur an overall bill of well over $400,000 after four years of tuition and living expenses.[22] Upon graduation, most people with these large graduate loans go on to make a lot of money, which they may then use to pay back the loans. Still, many of my lawyer and doctor clients feel burdened by and ashamed of these loan balances, even though there is nothing wrong with pursuing a tough degree. People with these loans did not necessarily make some shameful mistake; it's simply the reality of having advanced degrees.

Failed businesses: In 2020, I took on my first clients who had over $100,000 of debt. As it turns out, most people in this category aren't going on extravagant shopping sprees at Louis Vuitton or cruising the Caribbean. They're often hardworking entrepreneurs who fall victim to the fact that most businesses fail.

In 2023, CEO Jensen Huang of NVIDIA, a company currently worth more than $3 trillion in market capitalization, was asked what kind of company he would want to start today if he were thirty years old again. He immediately answered, "I wouldn't do it. Building a company... turned out to be a million times harder than I expected it to be."[23] Here is the leader of one of the ten most valuable companies in the world, telling others not to pursue entrepreneurship. Founding a successful company involves a little bit (or maybe a lot) of naiveté and belief that things will work out, that it can be done. In some ways, you almost want tunnel vision to tune out the many risks (regulatory, market, customer, competition) that can stand in the way of achieving your dream. Unlike Silicon Valley tech founders, who can raise millions of dollars of funding, most Americans self-fund their entrepreneurial dreams. A lawsuit or a bad year in the market could mean life or death for a company and hundreds of thousands of dollars lost. The people I coached who chose debt were emotionally tied to their companies and did not want to see them fail.

There is no need for shame for any of these people who fall into debt. Most people don't get married to get divorced. Most people don't go to school to make just a little more money. Most people don't start businesses to lose money. Even if your specific debt and situation were not mentioned in this section, you are not alone. While it can feel heavy to have debts in your life, one of the first attitudes I'd like you to take on as you read this chapter is this: You are not your debt.

Types of Debt

To slay the beast, you need to know its weakness. First, let's go over the most common types of debt and how they work so that you have this information as you create your debt-free plan.

Credit Card Debt: When a financial institution issues you a credit card, you use revolving credit to purchase things.[24] You usually have a grace period of about twenty to twenty-five days after the statement closes to pay your credit card bill. Once that period is over, any unpaid balance starts earning interest. For example, if you have a bill of $100 and you pay $80 by the end of the grace period, the remaining $20 will be added to your unpaid balance and will start earning interest. Credit cards charge an annual percentage rate (APR) applied monthly to outstanding balances. It's not unusual to see APRs of 20%

Month 1

Spend money

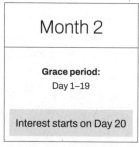

Month 2

Grace period:
Day 1–19

Interest starts on Day 20

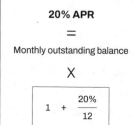

20% APR

=

Monthly outstanding balance

X

$$1 + \frac{20\%}{12}$$

or even 30%, an exorbitant amount to be paying on top of the principal amount. Credit card companies may offer a low introductory APR or no interest to attract new borrowers, but after the promotional period, these rates often rise quickly to double digits.

Personal Loans/Lines of Credit: Personal loans are unsecured loans offered by lenders where you offer no collateral. The loan has higher interest rates than secured debt. Usually, personal loans have lower interest rates compared to credit cards, and the rates are fixed upfront (usually in the 10%– 20% range). Unlike credit card loans, most personal loans have a due date, and the loan is amortized over the loan's lifetime so that the borrower has steady, monthly payments of the same amount.[25]

Student Loans: Over 90% of American student loans are federal loans.[26] Typically, a borrower can get better rates from the government than from private lenders, as well as some added benefits. Many federal loans are subsidized, meaning there is no interest while a student is in school. Furthermore, as seen during the COVID-19 crisis, the government can suspend payments on loans (deferment and forbearance) or cancel loans (forgiveness) altogether. As student loans are unsecured debt, interest rates are often in the 5%–10% range, which are lower than credit card and personal loans. A standard repayment plan lasts ten years. Borrowers can apply for a variety of programs from studentloans.gov that range from lowering payments based on income, deferring payments (meaning you delay loan repayment and interest accrues in the meantime), forbearance (meaning you delay loan repayment and interest does not accrue in the meantime), or even getting student loans forgiven. Forgiveness includes Public Student Loan Forgiveness (PSLF) for those who work in a qualifying job, and other cases, such as a student attending a fraudulent for-profit educational institution or a student loan servicer providing incorrect service.[27]

Mortgage Loans: Most Americans are unable to purchase a home all with an all-cash offer, so they turn to banks to take out mortgages, or real estate loans. The house is the collateral for a mortgage, so mortgages typically have the lowest interest rate of all loans an individual can qualify for. In most years, other than high-inflation periods, mortgage interest rates have been 1%–5%. A borrower typically pays a down payment; the standard that most homebuyers are recommended to pay is 20% of the home's value.[28] Most mortgages come in fifteen- and thirty-year terms. Suppose a mortgage loan has a fixed interest rate. In that case, the loan balance and interest are added over the term and divided into equal monthly payments.[29] If the interest rate is not fixed, monthly payments may vary as the Federal Reserve interest rate moves up and down.

Monthly mortgage payment
=

$$\text{Outstanding balance} \times \frac{\text{Annual interest rate}}{12}$$

Amortized over loan term

Car Loans: Similar to mortgage loans, car loans are another type of loan with collateral—in this case, the car. Like a mortgage, a car loan asks a borrower to place a down payment on the vehicle (though zero–down payment loans are also available), then the principal borrowed and the interest are amortized over the loan's lifetime. Most car loans are paid over a five-year period, and interest is usually fixed.[30] Cars almost always lose value over time, with very few exceptions.

Retirement Loans: Employer-sponsored retirement plans such as 401(k)s may offer you the ability to borrow against the money you've contributed and invested. Loans for 401(k)s are typically tied to your paycheck. These loans can be very misleading. Though many 401(k) plans advertise interest-free loans, the amount you borrow doesn't accumulate investment growth, and the payments for the loans are garnished from your paycheck. Making tax-deferred contributions to your 401(k) (meaning you don't pay taxes on the income you contribute to the 401(k) that saved you on income taxes on your paycheck) doesn't make up for the loan amount because 401(k) loan payments use after-tax income.[31] Finally, should you terminate employment with your employer, there's a possibility that the total amount is due upon termination.

Medical Debt: When medical bills exceed what an insurance company or patient can pay, they become medical debts. Most medical providers offer 0% interest payment plans, typically up to six months in length. However, after six months, many providers mark these medical debts as delinquent and sell them to a debt-collection company. Receiving calls from these companies can be distressing. However, if you find yourself in a situation where your debt has been taken on by such a firm, don't lose hope. You can negotiate with them. Most collectors don't pay the full price of your debt, so there is leeway for you. For example, a debt collector could have purchased your $5,000 debt for $1,000, but they may try to collect from you at full value to make a profit of $4,000.[32] Other collectors are paid out based on a percentage of debt collected. Negotiating debt typically negatively impacts your credit history, so weigh that as you consider what path to take.

Tax Debt: In the US, taxpayers file annual tax returns that determine whether the tax payments they made for the previous calendar year were accurate. The IRS has three years to assess whether taxes are owed and ten years to collect those taxes. The IRS also provides several relief programs to help you pay your taxes back. Typically, tax loans have low interest rates. However, suppose a borrower chooses to ignore tax bills. In that case, the IRS may ask your employer to pay the government your debt out of your future paychecks.

There are, of course, other types of debt than the ones I've described here, but these are some of the most common types. You'll see that most debts have something in common: They have a principal amount you borrowed, an interest rate, and a loan term or amount of time you have to pay the loan back in full. Hold on to this important concept, as we will revisit this later in the chapter to help you create your debt-free plan.

Money Root Cause and Debt

I provide the same advice for most people on paying down debt, but there are slight differences between root causes and how they lead to different ways to approach debt payoff. In this section, I outline a few steps for where you can start before you tackle your debt-free plan, which is described in detail at the end of this chapter.

Debt Advice for Feast and Famine

Step 1: Take the No-Spend Challenge.

Step 2: Use Trigger, Action, Reward to change your actions.

Step 3: Make spending harder.

Step 4: Use a twenty-four-hour freeze.

Step 1: Take the No-Spend Challenge.

For one week, challenge yourself to not spend on any nonessential items. You should still pay your housing bills, fuel your car, and feed yourself with groceries, but there ought to be (to the extent that is possible for you) no impulse or nice-to-have purchases.

As the days go on, you will probably start feeling triggered to spend. Write down what you're feeling and what is happening. Try to identify the specific trigger that led to that impulse. After seven days, you will have a written list of all the times you were tempted to spend, from which you can find patterns. Were there emotions you felt that were similar across the days? Is there a specific person who is causing you to buy something?

Step 2: Use Trigger, Action, Reward to change your actions.

You might be spending money to make yourself feel better without really thinking about the expense. Notice what your triggers are and what they're doing. Now change the action to something that addresses the trigger but without spending any money. If you are lonely, for instance, you can call or text a friend. Stressed? You can slow down and allow more time to focus on the work or life item causing you anxiety. Tired? You've overcommitted and need to rest. In this process, you will address and satiate the underlying need without spending money, and realize that in many cases, spending money in and of itself doesn't solve the underlying trigger or issue.

Step 3: Make spending harder.

As impulses are brain shortcuts, let's create a detour in your brain. If you have your credit card information saved in your online shopping accounts, for instance, you can simply delete your payment data from your account information. This forces you to get up to refer to your physical card each time you want to buy something. If you have your credit-card numbers memorized, you could call your card companies and ask to get a new card. You may be charged a small fee to do so, but it's worth it. Go to your online wallet, mobile wallet, or any online retailer you shop with, and delete your payment data from your profile. Go to all your subscriptions and pause whichever ones you can and then evaluate whether you are actively using them. Then go into your phone and computer and delete any apps and bookmarks aimed at spending money. This could range from payment apps like Venmo and PayPal to shopping apps like Target, Amazon, and Starbucks.

Here's the good news: You can always download these apps again if you really need them. But doing that extra step to place obstacles in front of opportunities to spend makes you think, *Wow, I need to put in extra effort to spend this money.* That simple action alone can help! Some personal finance educators recommend that you spend with just cash, which is something you can also try.

Step 4: Use the twenty-four-hour pause.

We want to give you more time to think about every purchase. Any time you want to buy something on impulse or that's nonessential, freeze that purchase for at least twenty-four hours. This includes shopping in person, when you find something at the store that was not on your original list. This helps you combat a very common "But it was on sale!" reasoning many people have. Stores and online shopping portals are designed to get you to buy without taking the time to think about whether you actually need or want that item. Having this twenty-four-hour rule in place gives you time to cool down and think about the purchase.

Debt Advice for Adverse Events

Step 1: "I am enough."

Step 2: Consider treating your mental health.

Step 3: Use Trigger, Action, Reward to change your actions.

Step 1: "I am enough."

When you experience Adverse Events, it can be difficult to separate your sense of self from your money habits. How you spend, what you spend on, and whom you spend on are all tied to your self-identity and feelings of worth. When a person who has experienced Adverse Events is asked not to spend on something, a part of their mind may backfire and scream, "This goes against everything I worked for!" If your self-worth is tied to purchasing, being asked not to buy something is akin to attacking who you are as a person as well as your sense of security.

There is a really great phrase I've learned that I'm going to ask you to repeat each time you feel unhappy about money: *I am enough—who I was, who I am, and who I will be.* I personally like chanting it while I'm crying into my afternoon energy drink. This amazing phrase acknowledges me as human, as a person, but it also takes away my dependency on affirmation. For Adverse Events, the trigger that causes you to spend usually has something to do with how you want yourself to be perceived and your self-worth to be defined. "I am enough" takes away the need to be defined using external factors.

Step 2: Consider treating your mental health.

Natalie grew up with strict parents who had high hopes for her. They didn't withhold money, but they were very controlling of her future and career. The family was well off, but because Natalie's parents were also immigrants, there were few luxuries because her parents wished to avoid credit card debt. Natalie grew up feeling she had to be perfect and get good grades so that she could eventually go to a good school and obtain a six-figure career in healthcare. Her parents made it clear that she couldn't end up working in a retail job, which doesn't pay as well. She shared with me, "I'm the oldest daughter, oldest cousin on both sides of the family. I think my parents had very high expectations of me. I had to hide parts of myself. I'm very critical of myself."

In college, across the country and away from the watchful eyes of her parents, Natalie's need for perfection unraveled. She didn't need to take out student loans—her parents helped pay for college—but she did it anyway to have money for herself. For the first time in her life, Natalie could be boisterous and loud! She could wear tight jeans and style her hair any way she liked. She wanted to buy and experience all the things she couldn't before. She wasn't worried about debt at the time, thinking that her healthcare career would eventually pay for it all. She took out $50,000 so she could feel free. Later, she financed her wedding with loans. She and husband at the time made more than $150,000 in combined income, yet their debt wasn't going away. It wasn't until a painful divorce (which didn't financially impact Natalie because they had no money to divide in the divorce) that she finally realized she had to change something to get debt-free. She started therapy, where she recognized that she could be her own person separate from her parents' hopes, and that person wanted financial freedom. She found that she wanted to travel, live life, and have every dollar accounted for. She wanted to be smart and aware of her money and also give to charity in the future.

Treating your mental health is probably the most essential step for addressing debt accumulated as a result of Adverse Events. For example, Natalie recognized that she was becoming too dependent on her ex-husband for her own happiness, so she began talk therapy. There are many modalities of talk therapy available to address different mental ailments. Furthermore, modern medicine continues to make breakthroughs in neuroscience, creating better, more targeted drugs that people can use to combat the symptoms of debilitating mental illnesses. If you have never treated your mental health, you might feel shame when signing up for a therapist or trying a medication. As someone who has experienced those feelings, I can tell you, there's nothing wrong with you as a person. We all need a little help sometimes. Don't rule out therapy or medication as a possible solution to what you are going through. Over time (anywhere from a few months to a few years), the goal for you is to allow the work of therapy, medicine, and self-work to diminish the effect that triggers have on your sense of self-worth.

Step 3: Use Trigger, Action, Reward to change your actions.

As you try out the first two steps, you will slowly learn to frame your world and finances less in terms of shame about your past and more in terms of affirming yourself. Your old spending cycle might have looked like this:

With more awareness and understanding of your triggers, you can change your actions to address your needs directly. Your new spending cycle might look like this:

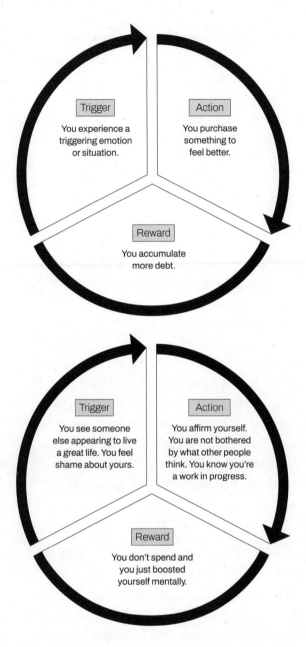

This is not easy at first. It took more than a year for Natalie to feel comfortable talking about her divorce, and to this day it's still painful for her to visit the topic. However, since she first worked with me, she has quadrupled her business income, bought a home, and reduced her loans by thousands of dollars.

Debt Advice for Scarce Immigrant

Most people with the Scarce Immigrant root cause don't come to me with significant consumer debt. They often grew up in frugal households and have been taught to avoid debt. The most common debt types they have, if any, are home mortgages and student loans. The latter are often unavoidable for many children of immigrants because these families see education as the key to upward socioeconomic mobility in their adopted country. According to the 2022 US Census, 45% of immigrants who arrived since 2010 have a bachelor's degree or higher, compared to 38% of American-born people.[33] Immigrant parents, however, might not be able to fund a college education, which is why they or their children need to rely on student loans.[34]

I also mention mortgages because I see a lot of home purchasing among immigrants and their families. I believe this is because a home is an asset they can see, and it feels less likely that it could be seized by an institution or a government. Take, for example, the collapse of Lebanon's economy. Following the 1975–90 civil war, the Lebanese government began taking on significant debt to run the country but made little money to meet the obligations. Most of Lebanon's national income came from tourism, foreign aid, its financial industry, and the support of surrounding allies and of its citizens who worked abroad and sent money home. Unfortunately, the Lebanese government never met its debt obligations, and when political strife erupted in 2019, foreign aid dried up and banks started denying depositors the right to withdraw money. The Lebanese pound lost 95% of its value as a currency. Lebanese people could no longer access their largely worthless savings accounts, and few people trusted in the government's ability to rectify the problem. These kinds of financial crises are not isolated. If someone witnesses an event where they're prevented from getting their own money from the bank, then what trust could they have in a financial institution in another country? Buying a home and paying down the mortgage feels more certain. One can always sleep in and touch the home, and it's not easily moved from one place to another. Being debt-free also makes one less reliant on institutions. Yet what they don't realize is that Scarce Immigrants are often so afraid of debt that they end up paying down debt too quickly.

What might a spending cycle look like for someone with a Scarce Immigrant root cause? The trigger is usually the fear of taking on debt. The

WEALTH IS A MINDSET

trigger or threat of debt often leads the person to either not spend at all, pay down a debt rapidly when they could better use those funds toward a potential opportunity, or refuse to make an investment that could pay off in the long run. My Wealth Diary, an online blogger tracking her journey to FIRE, shared with me how scared she felt six months into her first job when she realized she was responsible for paying off all her student loans.[35] She had grown up watching her parents worry about how they would make it financially from month to month. They never planned ahead or saved for a rainy day, much less for retirement. As a result, she got "tunnel vision... You want to get rid of everything. You want a sigh of relief, [like] 'I'm finally free.' " My Wealth Diary, like many others, played it safe. She was hyperfocused on paying off her debt, and in the process, she missed the opportunity to slow down and evaluate strategic ways to put more of her savings toward investments.

For the Scarce Immigrant root cause, the goal is less about getting on board with becoming debt-free and more about striking a balance between staying debt-free and investing when it makes sense. How do you know where to put your money?

Your Debt-free Plan

After you adjust your behavior based on your root cause, I want you to follow this ideal sequence for a debt-free plan:

1	Write down and organize your debts.
2	Save an emergency fund that can cover one month's essential expenses.
3	Start paying down your highest interest rate loans—paying more than the minimum—until you've eliminated all debt with interest rates of 10% and above.
4	Save a three-to-six-month emergency fund.

5	Start paying down your highest interest rate loans until you've eliminated all debt with interest rates of 5% and above.
6	If you have debts in collections, start negotiating those down to a settlement amount of less than half the original amount owed, ideally closer to one-third.
7	Pause. Now you can split your time between paying off debt with interest rates of 5% or less on time, and investing with the rest of your money.

Notice that in Steps 3, 5, and 7, I mention interest rates at specific ranges. What do *all* kinds of debt have in common that allows us to compare them? Their interest rate.

Most people categorize debts by type (for example, student loans versus credit card debt) and pay them off this way. I've even seen some people describe some debt as "good debt" and some as "bad debt." This description might have come from the fact that mortgages and student loans usually have lower interest rates than "toxic" credit card debt. However, this way of thinking about debt falls apart once we are in an environment where interest rates are changing. Debts are not necessarily on some moral scale of good versus bad. In 2022–23, leading up to my writing this book, the United States experienced unprecedented inflation, and the Federal Reserve stepped in by raising the federal interest rate. New mortgages had a 6% interest rate, car loans inched toward 10%, and credit card APR went over 30%. At these rates, no debt is considered "good." Instead, the most mathematically sound way to think about debt is to compare them to weeds growing in your backyard: The debts with the highest interest rates grow the quickest, and if you don't address those first, you'll soon have six-foot-tall weeds on your hands. The debts with the lowest interest rates grow more slowly, which gives you time to remove the weeds; at the same time, you can plant some flowers for Future You to enjoy or use some of your money on other, more productive ventures.

Step 1: Organize your debts.

The first thing you will need to do is write down and organize your debts. Take a deep breath, my friend, because this exercise is not fun. Please remember what I said at the beginning of the chapter: Your debt do not define you. Doing this exercise and seeing your debts on paper do not show you're a bad person, but doing it for the first time is usually a negative experience for most people. Remember, you're not alone.

Use the following table to record as much detail as possible. If you don't have some of the information, call your debt servicer or lender. You don't need all the details for debts in collections, which happens when the original creditor sends your debt to a third party to collect it.[36] Refer to page 210 of the appendix for more detailed information.

Name	Original balance	Current balance	Interest rate	Minimum monthly payment	Loan due date (if there is one)

Be patient because some loan servicers might take some time to reply to you. Remind yourself that you are collecting information so your debt-free plan can be effective. It may feel very overwhelming when you first do this; practically every person whom I've walked through this process has cried. That's okay. Cry it out. You're on your way to healing, and you are going to let this debt fall off your shoulders.

Step 2: Save for a one-month emergency fund.

For many people, debt is the result of living paycheck to paycheck and then getting sidelined by a single emergency. Unfortunately, we must accept that the unexpected can and will happen to everyone. (When it rains, it pours, right?) Car accidents, company layoffs, and a health flare-up are just a few of the countless ways lousy luck can manifest itself. Without an emergency fund—in cash, not invested assets—it is very easy for someone to fall back onto using credit cards or other loan products when they're in tough situations.

Don't overthink what bills qualify for the use of your emergency fund. You need a roof over your head, transportation, a phone connection, food, hygiene, and health. There are a lot of other things you can do without. Having even one month of funds for essential bills set aside helps break the paycheck-to-paycheck cycle. If you need help with this exercise, refer to page 211 of the appendix for more detail on what to include.

Step 3: Start paying off the highest interest rate loans of 10% and above.

You need to estimate how much you can pay each month toward debt. For most people, understanding the full picture of your expenses might take a few months, but we don't have time to waste. Using the illustrations on pages 213–14 of the appendix, you can estimate your monthly income and expenses, including your minimum payments. By doing so, you will have a starting point that gives you a sense of how much money you have at the end of each month to pay toward debt. You should have enough money to cover your must-have expenses and minimum payments, and you may be dialing back some of your nice-to-have expenses. If you don't have any extra money, then you will need to lower your expenses, raise your income, or both. Tracking your expenses, ideally every week, will give you better data for the future.

You want every extra dollar you have at your disposal to stretch. An extra dollar toward a debt with a high interest rate goes further than toward a debt with a low interest rate.[37] The debt-free plan is less about how much is owed on each obligation and more about how quickly it is growing. Once all your loans with 10% and higher interest rates are paid off, move to the next step.

Step 4: Save a three- to six-month emergency fund.

A larger emergency fund becomes more important once your debt is stabilized. (Interest rates between 5% to 10% are still high, but I don't consider this range to be dire.) Three to six months of emergency savings is standard because these savings can cover essential expenses in the event you lose your source of income or encounter unexpected circumstances, such as an unplanned medical expense. Most job searches also take three to six months to materialize.

I would recommend an emergency fund covering closer to six months if you are the primary breadwinner and provide for more than yourself (such as a spouse and children). It's easier for a single adult to pare back expenses, but if you have children or a partner depending on you, it can be a more significant challenge, with commitments that are hard to back out of.

Step 5: Pay down loans with 5% interest rate and above.

After beefing up your emergency fund to cover several months, return to paying down debt. Interest rates of 5% or higher still mean that the debt is growing quickly.

Step 6: Negotiate bills in collections.

By the time your debt is in collections, you might not need to pay the full amount. Your lender already made some interest off you, and the collections agency simply wants to recover something. At this point, you have enough experience to start saving larger chunks of money at a time. You need to save up a sum (or possibly dig it out of your emergency fund) for negotiations. This is because when you negotiate a debt, you're often asked to pay off the negotiated amount as a lump sum, so you'll need a chunk of change for that. Negotiating your debt here could help you save on your total repayment balance, but also keep in mind that it could negatively impact your credit score. Do not negotiate until you have fully weighed the pros and cons.

Step 7: Find a balance between investing and paying off debt with less than a 5% interest rate.

On average, investments in the US stock market grow around 8%–10% a year, but that is not guaranteed. Sometimes the investments can go negative before turning positive. Paying off debt means that you are ensuring, with 100% certainty, that this debt is no longer going to charge you another 5% or more of interest a year.[38] The reason why many personal finance experts and I set that threshold is because at 5%, the difference between paying down debt and investing evens out. Since investments in the US stock market don't guarantee a payout of 8%–10% compound interest a year, we dial back the expectations due to the uncertainty. Eight to ten percent with uncertainty is about equal to about 5% with 100% certainty. Thus, once your debts are below the 5% interest rate, then the scales reverse, and investing with uncertainty still beats paying off low-interest-rate debts with certainty.[39]

Now that you have all the steps for a debt-free plan, I want to mention there are a few exceptions to how you may make this work yourself.

- You need to get motivated. I get it. Some people need a small win. I think it's more than okay to start by paying off your smallest debt first, which is called the Snowball Method, as popularized by Dave Ramsey. The mental boost you can get is brilliant, but don't let it last forever. After about three months of debt payoff or after paying off your smallest loan, whichever comes first, I want you to switch to paying off the largest interest rate first, then move on to the next largest, which is called the Avalanche Method.

- If you want to skip Step 1, you can temporarily move back home with family. Not having to pay rent removes much pressure, and you can go straight to Step 2 if your family acts as your emergency fund.

- Your family is willing to give you a no-interest loan for some of your debts. Those debts should fall into the final step of the debt-free plan, meaning that you can invest more instead of paying down debt.

- You have a high-interest-rate debt, but it may be under some government-sponsored repayment program, like the ones offered for federal student loans. Oftentimes these programs allow you to make smaller monthly payments than originally owed, and for some individuals, the balance of the loan might be forgiven at the end of the loan. It might be worth underpaying a student loan to at least get yourself debt-free from the other loans that don't have such perks

Each person's debt-free strategy looks a bit different, but keep in mind that your plan is a combination of mental and financial work. The step-by-step outline above shows how you can work with the numbers. But remember that you are more than a number. Identify your root cause when it comes to debt, and use the steps suggested (including Trigger, Action, Reward) to rewire how you think about the spending that led to your debt. Consider therapy, if this is a part of the equation. Then, find at least one afternoon or weekend day where you organize your debt and start your debt-free plan. Commit to tracking your expenses going forward, spending at least one hour a week doing this. You will have a more accurate picture of your actual spending and your ability to pay down debt each month. Calculate and estimate how much you will pay (you can use the graphics in page 213 of the appendix). Adjust your expectations accordingly as well; if you can't consistently meet a specific debt repayment goal, pull back to something more realistic. As I said in Chapter Three, your goal must be 90% achievable.

It may feel overwhelming at first, but you can do it. When Maria first worked with me at the end of 2021, her net worth was around $16,000. This included:

Assets	Amount
Savings for herself	$5,700
Savings for her daughter	$3,300
Retirement savings	$19,000
Car	$12,000
Travel fund	$800

Liabilities	Amount
Student loans	$25,000

A few months later, she added a car loan of $44,000, and she moved out of her parents' home. Her essential expenses now were about $5,000 per month. Her car loan and her student loans both had interest rates of around 3.5%–4%, which were very reasonable. We also later found out that she might qualify under a special student loan forgiveness program because of a misleading advertisement by the for-profit education institution she attended. Her initial goal was to build her cash savings up to around $15,000 for a three-month emergency fund. I didn't push for six months for a few reasons, one being that she still had a support system nearby in the form of family, and two that she worked in a relatively stable industry. After she accumulated her emergency fund, I had her focus her extra money toward investing for retirement. She was still making the required minimum payments on her student and car loans, but we weren't in a hurry to pay them off early. She applied for student loan forgiveness, and we still haven't heard back yet. Maria also worked on getting promoted at work and increased her income by 50% since 2021.

In July 2024, she updated me with the following snapshot of her net worth.

Assets	Amount
Saving for a home down payment	$3,000
Savings for her daughter (both general savings and college)	$8,500
Retirement savings (consisting of a 401(k) and Roth IRA)	$81,000
Emergency fund	$15,500
Travel fund	$1,600
Value of her new car	$28,000

Liabilities	Amount
Student loans	$17,000
Car loan	$29,000

Her total net worth had increased from $16,000 to $92,000 in just two and a half years. By understanding that her loans were not urgent, the power of investing in the stock market had paid off handsomely for her. The transformation was breathtaking. Maria, for the first time in her life, felt wealthy.

CHAPTER SIX

YOUR CAREER IS NOT YOUR IDENTITY

Here's a hard-hitting truth I had to learn: Following your "passion," especially early in your career, is not good advice. Most people would stop working if they didn't need the money. Finding a job that you *love*, that is everything you could ever want, is very difficult. And having it pay well? That's a dream attained by a privileged minority. We hear a lot of "follow your passion" speeches at college graduations because they are given by celebrities, leading academics, businesspeople, and athletes who get to do what they love and make a lot of money for it. Imagine graduating with an expensive diploma in hand and being told that you must find something you love to do, but you have already taken whatever offer you could find during your job search. Now what? Was that a mistake? Most of us mortals must shoulder the reality that we have bills to pay and mouths to feed, even if it's just our own.

I wish I'd heard this advice at my own commencement: Find a career that pays you well enough *in the moment,* for the skills you currently have and those you want to develop.

You Are Not Your Job

Can we take a moment to examine the idea that our jobs define our identities? In many highly industrialized countries, particularly the US, when you meet someone for the first time, one of the first questions you ask or are asked is, "What do you do for a living?"

When I think of my best and closest friends, I don't think of them as the best neurosurgeon in the field or the person who got laid off last year. Being a neurosurgeon is certainly impressive, and being laid off can be upsetting, but that's not why I choose to be friends with someone. My friends are the ones who stood up for me when I was being bullied, or who texted me when I was down about my love life. Remembering how I love them for who they are, and the relationships we've built together, was vital for me to uncouple my identity from my work in the context of a very individualistic, work-driven culture.

It also doesn't make sense to base yourself and your human value on your work output, especially during job transitions or career changes. Our work culture constantly pressures us to keep climbing the ladder or search for a better position, presenting this as the best way to succeed. LinkedIn further cements the practice by announcing promotions, milestones, and accomplishments. What happens if it lands you in a place where your health is affected? Or worse, what happens when it all goes away?

When I moved to New York City after getting married, I pursued one of my life's dreams: to work for a well-known fashion company. It all appeared so glamorous to me. Retail was my favorite business topic to learn about whenever I read the newspaper, and many of the female leaders I looked up to during business school managed retail brands and companies. I loved fashion, and New York City was the fashion capital. I jumped into a corporate strategy job at one of the most prestigious mass retail lingerie brands in the world. Having a sexy brand on my resume garnered a lot of wide-eyed smiles from anyone who met me. Furthermore, it was a Fortune 500 company, which meant job stability, good healthcare benefits, annual salary raises that were in line with inflation, and a great employee discount. It felt like my life's dream of becoming a corporate leader was settling into place. All those late nights doing impossible problem sets, the hours I spent on extracurriculars instead of sleeping, even the bullying

I endured as a nerdy high schooler, they were justified because I was on my way to my dream career.

But my dream quickly turned into a nightmare. My bosses were both micromanagers, and I just didn't fit into the appearance-driven, emotionally charged culture. I ended up extremely miserable at this toxic job. Nothing I did was ever good enough, a lot of my work got changed and picked apart, and sometimes I would even get dropped from meetings I thought I was supposed to attend. There were days I spent crying the moment I got home, and I took all criticism and feedback personally, believing I was a failure and not cut out for this kind of work. I had such low self-esteem that my husband suggested that I consider working somewhere else. However, given my ambitious nature, I was afraid that if I left my job, I would be an even bigger failure. I wanted to make things right, please my bosses, turn things around and give them my best effort, all because I prided myself on my work ethic and would do anything to change people's opinions of me. In my manic drive to have my "revenge" on my childhood bullies, I had unwittingly started chasing a new form of affirmation to replace the loneliness I had felt as a child. I wanted to do well at my job because that would validate all my hard work and my expensive education.

What I had trouble seeing was that the behavior of my bosses was reflective of the overall culture at this company. As I began making friends through different departments, I heard similar stories of mistreatment. None of the people I met felt they had any ability to advocate for themselves in the workplace, and many of them had no friends in different departments due to the siloed nature of the work organization. I also began sharing some of my day-to-day experiences with my college and MBA friends, and several of them pointed out that while all corporations had their downsides, my experience seemed to be worse than most. All signs pointed to my needing to leave instead of trying to fix the situation. Had it not been for my fantastic therapist, who is worth her weight in gold, I probably would have stayed even longer at this company, thinking that I could fix its inherent toxicity. It took me two and a half years to leave this job.

I was very grateful to return to the world of management consulting after my stint with the lingerie company. I now knew how to identify toxicity. Then came the next lesson: how to value myself beyond my work. I embraced consulting fully. The work was something that I was pretty good at, and I got to learn about a number of industries quickly, work with large amounts of data, and meet executive-level people. Additional perks included good pay, prestige, fun office events, smart coworkers, and the opportunity to move into leadership roles. Once again, I fell into the alluring trap of defining myself by my career. Consulting was the stamp of approval I thought I needed for my expensive degrees to be "worth it." Though by this time I was already a couple years into the extreme frugal journey my husband and I had agreed upon, I wasn't fully convinced that I mattered outside of work. Keep in mind, our saving at the time was only to serve for a long, unpaid maternity leave, and I had always assumed that I would continue working afterward.

Everything came to a head with my first bad performance review. I was a part of a project that required a far more advanced financial model than was initially presented to the client. As my team created the model, I missed several instances where I should've stepped in and simplified it or communicated more clearly to my bosses why the work would take longer than expected. Having a lousy review crushed me beyond belief. I was giving countless hours to this company, I wasn't seeing my husband much, and the only time my friends and I got to meet up was crammed into short brunches and dinners on the weekends. Sometimes I was so busy that I would try to take care of personal errands virtually, in between work calls, on a small screen hidden in the corner on my computer. If I wasn't considered a good performer at work, then what did I have left? I gave this company everything. Did my life even matter after this?

My therapist pointed out that this intensity was neither normal nor healthy. For a few months, I had to talk myself up to regain my confidence and sense of self. I repeated words of affirmation: "You are smart. You are capable." This positive self-talk helped me pull myself out of the scarcity mindset from that performance review, which had me thinking that my professional life was over. I had to remind myself that my kindness, friendships, and marriage were more important than my performance at work.

When I had my first child, I realized that the journey I'd taken to get to this point in my career was soul-sucking. The fancy dinners, pleasant hotel stays, five-figure bonuses, and small words of praise I once hung onto were just the wires of a cage to keep my spirit and heart trapped inside. And not outside where they belonged. Finally, I truly understood that I'd earned the freedom my husband and I dreamed of, but I was doing nothing to enjoy it.

I share all this because it illustrates the seductive power of making a stable job the purpose of one's existence and the justification for personal sacrifice. I gave the majority of my waking hours to work, to the point where it began to feel like a religion, like a life that I had to live in order to be a valid person. It takes a lot of internal work to decouple that dependency. That decoupling must happen when we want change, such as a mental health break, a promotion, a career change, more income, or all of the above.

Identifying a Toxic Work Situation

What does toxicity at work look like? Generally, it's when you do not feel you are being treated like a human being. Some examples could include:

- Having little to no control over your scheduling, even though the expectation upfront was that you should have flexibility

- Not being included in the meetings and discussions you need to attend in order to get critical information for your job, or not being given the resources you need to work effectively

- Being punished for attending to your personal life, such as medical appointments and family emergencies

- Feeling that you cannot be honest or your authentic self around your coworkers or boss for fear of retaliation

- Feeling pressured or manipulated into doing things that go against your value system

- Being promised certain benefits or rewards, only to have them unfulfilled or removed without cause

The straightforward answer to how to resolve a toxic work situation is to leave. You can't stay and fix it. Why is that? Toxicity, as with other aspects of a company's culture, often comes from the top, and company leadership is powerful—and usually the last to get fired. So, if leadership doesn't change, the company doesn't change. One must also be careful about bringing these issues to human resources, which is controlled by leadership. I once saw a coworker being pushed out of the company despite doing good work because she didn't get along with her boss. She went to HR to try to address their differences, and within a week I was outside sitting on a cement bench with her, patting her back as she cried about being let go.

How are toxic work cultures created? Reed Hastings, the founder of Netflix, said, "The *real* company values, as opposed to the nice-sounding values, are shown by who gets rewarded, promoted, or let go."[40] When there is a culture mismatch between you, the employee, and the people whom the company promotes, there's a greater likelihood that you will experience toxicity and appear to be the outcast. Remember, when you experience toxic behavior—especially from a boss or from coworkers—it is much more a reflection on them than on you. At the lingerie brand, my bosses often told me I was being manipulative, not doing work correctly, and not being sensitive. In reality, insensitivity came from leadership, as I often observed executives ignoring the overwhelming feedback from customers that the brand's values were out of touch and not evolving with the times, and I was merely the messenger who was reporting the truth. I don't think my bosses were being intentionally mean; they were just operating in an environment that rewarded malignant behavior at every level, from the bottom to the top.

However, toxic situations at work affect your personal mental health, which leads to other adverse outcomes, some of which can impact your personal finances. For the sake of your financial health, the environment must change.

How to Move Forward Mentally

Let's say you just received a bad performance review after giving all your time and energy to your job. Or perhaps a coworker or manager accused you of being the reason why something was not successful. Or maybe you fell into a personal conflict with a coworker and it's affecting your ability to do your job.

The first thing to do is to get your feelings out in a safe space. When I get home from work, I let out all my anger, frustration, indignation, disappointment, and loss. When my husband isn't home, I vent openly to myself. It's important for us to experience our emotions in the moment because they are powerful and can cause damage if we keep them bottled up. Afterward, I like to get a good night's sleep, giving my body and brain a rest before I decide what to do next. In most cases, I lean toward action as my next step. If I experience something negative at work, in order to change it, I must do something different. I try to focus on what I'm able to do, but I also have to recognize there are things not under my control. For example, as a parent of a young child, I will always have less time to dedicate to my career than those who do not have children, and that's a limit I just have to work with.

How we are viewed at work has to do more with how our work is perceived than the actual work. If I receive a bad performance review, my goal then is to read my review without emotion and understand what my superiors perceive about the subpar performance. Then, I talk to someone who is successful at work to see how they would approach my situation. Typically, successful people at work know whom to talk to, how to present a challenging situation, how to win people over to their cause, and what resources are best to use.

For work conflicts, it might help to speak to someone neutral to get their read on the situation. If this coworker is very experienced, that can be helpful as well, as they may have seen similar situations in the past and can help you figure out if your conflict is something that happens often or is unusual.

Finally, remember that you are worthy, no matter what you do at work. Just like it took my repeating religiously, "You are smart. You are capable," to myself every morning, it's important to note that your life at work is not your entire life. Bosses and companies come and go. You have a rich life to live outside of work—and that's what financial freedom is all about.

Root Causes and Careers

Your money root cause can also manifest in how you build your career. After all, there are many unspoken rules in every industry. If you don't know these rules, navigating it may be more challenging for you than for someone who understands what they must do and thus appears to fit in more. I want to take this part of the chapter to help you make small changes to how you approach your career to set yourself up for success.

Career Tips for Feast and Famine

If you've experienced Feast and Famine, you often need a total lane shift when it comes to careers. The Feast and Famine root cause is often associated with families that make low to average income, and it can be hard for people from this background to imagine a future that could be different. Many people with this root cause often tell me they don't feel they belong with people who have a lot of money. They don't know what to do in a situation where most others around them come from wealth and privilege. This is because someone with the Feast and Famine root cause often did not grow up with an adequate support system to help them explore high-earning careers.

My client Ayana grew up with her parents in unstable financial situations, living in neighborhoods that had mostly low-income families like hers. Her father was a janitor while her mother stayed at home, and bills never got paid on time. Consequences ranged from the electricity being cut off to the family being evicted from their home. Ayana recalled they stayed at "homeless shelters and missions a few times. There was a lot of moving. It was pretty traumatic."

Ayana received a prestigious scholarship that covered ten years of secondary education, which could have paid for medical school if she'd wanted. But she struggled in school because of stress at home, and as a result, she dropped her pre-med requirements, graduated college, and began working as a research coordinator. Her dream of becoming a doctor "went down the drain." A few years later, Ayana decided that culinary school was her calling. Her scholarship wouldn't cover culinary school, however, so she took on loans. By the time we worked together, she wasn't making enough money as a chef to cover even the minimum payments on her loans.

No one who grows up low-income wants to stay that way. Ayana's mother even explicitly said she expected Ayana to "grow up, get rich, and put [her] in a really nice house." She could have left her family behind to go to college. However, she was convinced she had to stay with her parents to keep things together. She didn't let herself dream of a different future. When she finally decided to go to culinary school, it was a far cry from her original medical school dreams, but it was an act of rebellion because she had denied herself so much by staying at home with her parents. She wanted to do something that made her happy. She had no one to caution her that few chefs made above-average income and that she would struggle to pay back her student loans.

People with the Feast and Famine root cause don't normally receive a lot of support and guidance when they are seeking well-paid jobs. There may be hopes and dreams of doing well, but because the parents often didn't have the tools to excel in their careers, they don't know how to coach their children in this way. There can be this mindset of "I grew up low-income, so I guess my life will be of the same as my parents." If you do think this way, having a singular focus on moving your career into the fast-moving lane is essential, but you also need good guidance.

Eventually, my coaching and other events in her life led Ayana to recognize she needed more job stability. She pivoted to working a full-time job with benefits in a space she loved—educational coaching, an area that encompassed her passions for connecting with people, being creative and innovative, and contributing to the lives of children. Ayana recently told me she was now making "the best salary of my life, with good health insurance! I'm finally in a place where I can think about getting my finances together. I want to be out of debt, and I want to think about myself."

If you relate to the Feast and Famine root cause, rely on the perspective and lived experience in this book and do one of the following: increase your earnings, augment your skillset, or jump to a new industry. You can and will live a different life than your parents did. If you need additional resources and support, consider hiring a career coach who has helped place a lot of people into your desired field and join networking events where you can meet people in new industries (more on that in the next chapter). These actions can help you approach your next job more thoughtfully.

Career Tips for Adverse Events

Toxicity breeds toxicity, and if you have the Adverse Events root cause, you risk landing in a poisonous work environment and sticking with that situation for a long time. Like your upbringing, you might not have experienced anything other than negativity, so you may not even be aware that your workplace is unhealthy to begin with.

My client Sammie grew up being abused by her father, who blamed her for their poverty. Out of shame for living in low-income housing, he took out his anger and frustration on her, which led to violent abuse fueled by alcoholism. Sammie quickly learned that she "wasn't worthy" of having money. As an adult, she stuck with a high-stress job because she never wanted to depend on anyone else. It was normal for her to feel like her needs and her health didn't matter as long as she was making money. She would work long hours at prestigious global companies, building her expertise in marketing and sales. Sammie also became romantically involved with an abusive person to whom she gave all her savings to help support his business, which eventually failed. Sammie ignored all the warning signs around her life until one day, in her thirties, she went to the emergency room with vomiting, dizziness, and migraines, which turned out to be a brain tumor.

Luckily, Sammie was able to have most of the growth removed and stabilized, but she still felt "anger, guilt, depression, fear, and anxiety. I struggled to find my footing in a world that suddenly seemed unfamiliar. Self-isolation became my norm, when all I wanted was to reclaim a sense of normalcy." When I began working with Sammie, she was in her forties and years into her healing journey. She saw how the stress of where she was working and the relationships she had stayed in were taking the life out of her, driving her to give money to others instead of investing in herself, which also made her feel like she was trapped in a series of bad situations. She was done giving herself to greedy corporations and people. Instead, Sammie started working for herself and started on a path toward prioritizing her own happiness. On one breezy and humid spring day, I happened to be vacationing where Sammie lived, and so we got together for lunch. She pulled up in an old Chevy Malibu, proudly laughing at that the fact that her car was still running. Despite her residual medical difficulties, Sammie was full of joy. While I sweated it out on a sunny patio with a steaming hot plate of beef and eggs, she excitedly told me about all the things I should do to explore her town, all the new friends she had met, the community she learned to lean on to build her business and make more than $200,000 a year, and her health. She dreamed of early retirement and a slow-paced, hearty life.

Sammie was fortunate to reach a place where she was mentally and emotionally ready to make changes. It is imperative to understand that toxicity thrives on your not having a great sense of self and your willingness to sacrifice a large part of who you are for the company. These workplaces often create a combative, competitive, secretive environment that makes it hard to see transparently that you are not being treated well. If you relate to the Adverse Events root cause, ask yourself daily: Is my workplace, or my boss, prioritizing my psychological and emotional well-being? Is this job serving my goals and not harming my mental health? If the answers to both questions are no, then you're in a toxic environment.

A few steps that can help you cope with a toxic workplace include focusing on your mental and physical well-being. Committing to therapy or taking up a gym class can provide more support to your brain. Talk to someone removed from your situation who can help you better see whether your situation is normal. This could be a friend or a career coach.

Career Tips for Scarce Immigrant

Sometimes, parents with the Scarce Immigrant root cause make it almost impossible for their children to branch out independently. Whenever I face a career change, I think about how often my Chinese parents pointed out that being a doctor or engineer was the best way to be financially stable, and how differently my life turned out from that. Those little phrases can stay with you for a long time. Many of the rigid, institutional steps I took since I made the manifesto in my teenage years were actually born out of a Scarce Immigrant mindset, where failure was not an option. My parents sacrificed so much, and they wanted to see me succeed. Becoming a doctor or an engineer was, in their mind, a surefire way to guarantee that because it was prestigious and highly paid. In high school, I began cracking under that pressure when I was no longer the best person at math (we had not one but two people in my class who made it to the national Math Olympiad team that year). So, in college, I thought management consulting seemed like the perfect compromise in return for my never carrying a stethoscope or learning about thermodynamics, my dad's favorite topic as a mechanical engineer.

When I branched out as an entrepreneur, I kept one foot in the corporate world, just in case. I also maintained my wedding photography business as a side hustle for ten years. When I joined the world of technology startups in San Francisco, I picked what appeared to be an established company. Though I wanted to devote more time to Save My Cents, I held back for six years because I didn't think that being a personal finance educator had any prestige or money attached to it. But when I finally quit the corporate world to run Save My Cents full-time, my husband said to me, "I'm surprised you lasted this long in both management consulting and corporate work. You were born to be a hustler and business owner." I never recognized my own proclivities because I was so focused and conditioned by my immigrant upbringing to do the right thing, to check all the boxes for my career. I never believed I could do things differently.

Sometimes the best career choices feel the opposite of what feels safe to us. While now I have little to no security on the income I make from Save My Cents, I am grateful for every cent that I do have. I am joyful. I feel the most like myself. For me, being an online personality means I don't have to hide my snarky yet sunshine-y personality; it could be a part of my branding. Oh yeah, and while I am my own boss, I know not to be too hard on myself.

The point is that it never hurts to experiment with jobs, through side hustling, internships, or moonlighting, to at least get a feel for what else is out there. I also think it's okay to stay at your full-time job to keep an income as you try new things, as long as you recognize that you'll be sacrificing your sleep and personal time. Who knows, maybe as you navigate your experiences at work, you may eventually come to the conclusion that you wish to leave, either by transferring to a different role or leaving the job or industry altogether. How would you do that? The next chapter will help you figure out your next steps and increase your income at the same time.

CHAPTER SEVEN

RAISING YOUR INCOME

A major frustration for some people on financial journeys is that they need more savings. There is only so much you can realistically do to cut your expenses. Everyone needs to spend on housing of some kind, be it rent or mortgage. Everyone has to get around via transportation. Food, drink, healthcare, clothing, internet and phone access, and childcare are just a few of the things that exist across every budget I've ever seen. If you're alive, you need money.

For income, though, the sky is the limit. Have you heard the concept of income being infinite? It truly is! Of course we have billionaires, but even coming down from the extreme, I know of salespeople who make close to $1 million a year through commissions. I know many business owners who easily clear more than $300,000 a year in payouts to themselves. I have had clients who moonlight as bartenders and yoga studio instructors to help pay off debts. It's possible for most people to work smarter to make more money.

For most of us, an increase in income must come from our jobs (though there are other ways to increase income that we will discuss later). It can also be tempting to create a new business, start a social-media venture, or rustle up a side gig to increase your revenue; I'll talk about those too, but know that starting a business is super difficult! Getting a job with a company or organization that will pay you more than you're making now, or even simply asking for a raise at your current job if you're due for one, is usually the "safer" route from an emotional standpoint. I encourage you to start by increasing your nine-to-five earnings. It can be as simple as switching teams or departments within the same company, or working more hours if you're hourly, and it doesn't have to be a wholesale industry change. Whatever you do, don't stand still and do nothing. Doing something, anything, to move your career forward is almost always better than maintaining the status quo. Networking, approaching a job search like an investor, negotiating your compensation, and positioning yourself for promotions can all help raise your income.

How to Network

For many people, the word "networking" usually conjures up images of stuffy meeting rooms filled with people in obnoxious suits, holding little cocktails with little napkins, making boring small talk about a particular industry. Networking can actually be quite fun. *What?* you may be asking. Yes—if you're just learning to network, you're hanging out with your favorite people: your friends. And most people wouldn't mind seeing a bestie occasionally in real life.

Most of my work experience has been in the United States. Here, it's often whom you know, not what you know, that is the make-or-break factor in one's career. Whenever you read biographies of famous and successful Americans, pay close attention to how they were introduced to so-and-so and how that allowed them to get their next big break. They may have come from wealthy and stable backgrounds (for example, Bill Gates's family was upper middle class, and Warren Buffett's father was a stock trader), which gave them more opportunities than the average person to meet people who could help them become successful. Or they could be someone who didn't grow up with any money or connections, but they met a few key individuals who made their careers happen (like Oprah, who worked her way up in network TV and credited a lot of her success to meeting the poet Maya Angelou). In the world of personal wealth, your network influences your net worth. While we shouldn't see our friends as dollar signs, they can significantly help us in our careers. After all, your friends care about you and want to help you.

Usually, companies already have certain candidates in mind before they ever post a job, if they even post it at all. When job searching for mid-senior corporate roles, I worked almost exclusively with corporate recruiters in confidential searches for job listings you wouldn't find on the company's website. It became clear to me that there was a particular dance I needed to follow to even be considered for such positions. If you're not from the specific background these recruiters are looking for, you must know someone who can vouch for you and convince the hiring manager that you are the best person for this high-ranking job.

I first learned how to network while still in college, then had the opportunity to practice and hone my skills throughout my career. The steps to networking are simple:

- Start with whom you know.
- Listen first. Don't worry about asking for things or taking something from the other person from the outset.
- Give more than you receive.
- Reap the rewards.

It sounds straightforward, but there are nuances to each of these steps, which I'll walk you through in detail.

Step 1: Start with who you know.

Think of your professional network like the layers of an onion. There is an inner core that you build around. We all start with the inner circle, Layer 1. Networking relies significantly on your innermost circle—your family and the people you break bread with. When I was first building my network, my Layer 1 included all my friends from college as well as the colleagues who began working with me in management consulting. Those of you with a large family can count your siblings, cousins, aunts, and uncles in your network. You should know what each person in this layer does for a living. You should feel comfortable texting or writing them at any time and be confident they will reply to you.

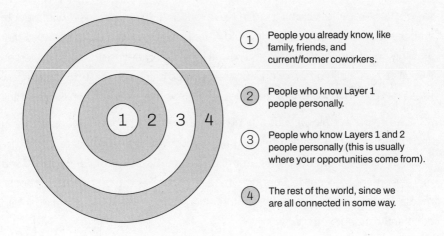

1 People you already know, like family, friends, and current/former coworkers.

2 People who know Layer 1 people personally.

3 People who know Layers 1 and 2 people personally (this is usually where your opportunities come from).

4 The rest of the world, since we are all connected in some way.

From this circle, you are going to expand to coworkers, former coworkers, acquaintances, and friends of friends. When you network, you would ideally gravitate toward meeting people in your industry who do the work you do or would like to be doing. For example, there was a time in my life when I considered starting a business related to construction. As part of my networking, I contacted friends working in architecture, industrial design, and construction to introduce myself to more people in this field.

You want to use Layer 1 to actively build Layer 2. You can do this by using what is called a double-blind "warm" introduction: First, ask your friend (Layer 1) if they'd be up for introducing you to the person you wish to meet (Layer 2). Write a few sentences describing yourself and what you want to do and share that with your friend. You could say something like, "I'm trying to work on solving XYZ problem and would like to bounce ideas with someone who knows the space. Do you know anyone I could speak to?" or "I've been wondering about switching into X industry and would love to learn more to get the lay of the land. I think you know someone who works in it. Do you think you could introduce me?" Your Layer 1 people want you to succeed and will try to be helpful and facilitate that introduction. Just be thoughtful and respectful when asking to meet others. Then, your friend will separately reach out to the other person and ask if they're open to meeting you. If they say yes, your friend will put both of you in contact with each other.

Once introduced, move quickly to find time to meet with this new person. Schedule around their availability and make it easy for them to say yes to you. For example, when I lived in New York and wanted to meet with people who were management-level, I would have breakfasts with them because that was the only time they were free. Typically, the first meeting would be in person if you live near each other, or on a phone or video call. Your goal is to get to know these people on a personal level, so quality one-on-one interaction is important.

If you get along with this person, they may become friends with you and move closer to Layer 1 over time. How do you develop this relationship? Well, by being a friend! Invite them to things. Send them funny texts and memes and holiday cards. Support whatever they're doing on LinkedIn or social media. People can move between the layers, which means your network can constantly change and grow.

Step 2: Listen—don't initially take.

For your first meeting with a Layer 2 person, be prepared with some general questions, such as what their background is, and specific questions that you'd like their help with. People can reveal information the company may not publish online. Get some insider secrets if you can! Before I meet new people, I look up their careers on LinkedIn or Google and try to become familiar with their work. I come up with a few questions I'd like answered, which could be about:

- Discovering how a new industry works
- Finding out the culture of a specific company
- Understanding the role and responsibilities of a job I have never heard of
- Learning how someone did something that I want to do as well
- Asking someone what not to do when I'm considering something specific
- Discussing the pros and cons of a decision
- Exploring compensation expectations and tips for navigating the job application process

Generally, I avoid asking in the first meeting if someone is comfortable offering me a job or becoming an involved mentor in my career (which is what I mean by "don't initially take"). While you are gathering information and getting to know someone, don't ask the person to do something that takes up a lot of their time or resources or comes across as a significant favor. It may make you appear desperate and needy. Instead, recognize that you are taking up someone's busy time and get to know them and get them to know you as a person first.

Step 3: Give more than you receive.

An essential thing to note here is that you shouldn't expect networking to get you a job immediately. New connections may open up to you by sharing a bit about themselves, but you still have a lot of work to do before that first conversation leads to a job offer.

As your layers expand, you'll need a way to keep in contact and stay updated with your network. LinkedIn right now remains the best professional tool for that. When I meet someone new, I ask afterward if we can connect on LinkedIn and add them as a connection. I also write down their email address and save a few notes from our conversation. For example, when I first began writing this book, I reached out to people with writing and publishing experience for advice and recorded what they said in a folder of notes for this book. After such meetings, remember to send a thank-you note to follow up, especially if the person went out of their way to help you learn about something you're unfamiliar with.

Now, take out time every week to dole out praise and goodwill, like an everyday Santa. When your connections get promoted or share good job news, congratulate them. If they announce a personal milestone, be supportive. If they post on LinkedIn asking something like finding a connection to someone or seeking advice, and you're in a position to help, help them. This is where you build up goodwill, or "social capital," as people in business school like to call it. Your generosity and kindness are the currency that you will draw upon in the future.

Step 4: Reap the rewards.

The best time to network is when you do not need a job. You're more likely to be relaxed, and people like catching up with colleagues who aren't always asking for something. Putting effort and time into networking at least once a week allows me to have a rich network. During job searches, my networking intensifies, often amounting to multiple chats a day. To keep track all of this, I take notes using a spreadsheet like the one below. I include a column for quick notes where I write down what I may need to follow up with, like sending someone my resume or asking for another introduction.

Once you've met with someone, you need to be diligent in following up with them on any promises or action items that came out of the meeting. People can get busy and forget about what they said they'd do to help you. When I write someone to introduce myself, I also remind myself to reach out to them in about a week to see what comes of it.

Name	Contact	Company	Title	Quick Note
Shang Saavedra	info@savemycents.com	Save My Cents, Inc.	CEO	

Is all this a lot of work? Absolutely! But it pays off, resulting in better, higher-paying jobs and exciting roles down the road.

Job Search like an Investor

Long gone are the days when people spent their entire lives with one company. Today, most of us increase our earning power and drive career growth through job hopping. You see, companies want you to stay stagnant. To keep profitable, business leaders count on employees to be relatively unaware of what else is out there, placating them with small increases in compensation over time that are often tied to hard-to-meet performance metrics. Most average companies operate like this; only the best ones with plenty of capital go all out and reward high performers. Job hopping is your best strategy to break free of this system of corporate stagnation.

I don't believe in allowing company executives that much power over my earning potential. Suppose I dedicate over two thousand hours a year to working. That time must be well compensated with dollar signs. We don't owe of them loyalty since most of them are not similarly loyal to their workforce. And as quickly as I can be cut from a job, I will just as easily walk away from a career that doesn't serve me. I'm a mercenary and work for hire.

How do you find a new job? Ideally, you want to go where there is more money and a high likelihood of rapid income growth. In some ways, you have to think like someone who would invest in that new industry or company. Here are concrete actions you can take to find a better and higher-paying job.

Evaluate the industry.

Avoid going into a dying industry or business. If the industry's prospects don't look good or lack investment, then most likely you'll continue to fight for dwindling jobs and stagnant pay. Instead, aim for a stable or growing sector. You can find out quickly how an industry is doing from reading the news and asking people working in that industry.

Identify key companies.

Create an ideal list of corporations in this industry with offices or openings where you live or offer remote opportunities. An internet or job board search can help generate this list. Focus on companies that are competitive and growing— ones with better products and services, good reputations, strong technology, a dominant market share, more capital, or some other competitive advantage. Investors like winning companies, and the more funding a company has, the more likely it can pay its employees well.

Learn the role and responsibilities.

Suppose you have a well-defined skill or career, like an accountant, salesperson, or engineer. In that case, it's easy to transfer your abilities to a new industry as long as it has similar roles to what you've worked in before. As someone with a more generalized set of skills, figuring out where I fit in a new organization often takes some sleuthing. I would talk to my network to understand the structure of the company, the main functions, how they worked together, how vital each function was, and what they did. I would mention to my network what my skillsets are and ask them where they think I might fit in at the new organization. If there's a job posting, be sure to read the description carefully, as this gives you the best initial view of what is expected of you if and when you are hired.

In some cases, if you are transitioning between roles, you may be advised to hone some of your expertise to match the new industry. This may involve trying to learn more about how to apply it or showcasing a project where you highlight how it can be used. For example, when I first applied to the corporate job at the lingerie company, I had very little retail experience, as I had consulted only for biotechnology companies. To prove that I could transfer that experience to retail, I put together a set of customer data and viewpoints and crafted a PowerPoint with brand strategy recommendations for my final interview. I knew that it made me stand apart from the pool of candidates.

In addition, you want to be able to match your skillsets to functions and areas where a company is willing to pay well. Let's say that you are a visual artist. A company that uses a lot of visual effects in their products, such as an established video gaming studio, would highly value those skills. But if you were at an accounting firm, your skillset is not how that firm makes money, thus you wouldn't likely be among the highest compensated employees. This dynamic between the type of company and its most prized assets is something I have often emphasized to people who want a rockstar trajectory. If you want your career to develop quickly, your skills need to be highly valued.

Find the hiring manager and get to know their hiring process.

Some job postings will note the name of the recruiter at the bottom to whom you submit your application. Some job postings are not as clear-cut. Going the extra step to identify the hiring manager can help your application stand out and ensure it is being considered by the decision maker. Furthermore, if you are invited to be interviewed, it's a good idea to ask for the name of the hiring manager and anyone else who is interviewing you for the next step.

Every company has its own way of interviewing, from brain teasers to strategy decks to coding challenges. Like a good investor, you should approach any job search by knowing the process. Ask or research the following:

- How many interviews can be expected?

- With whom are interviews conducted? What is the seniority of the people who are interviewing you?

- What do they like to understand in the interviews? Are there case studies, challenges, or other take-home-style assessments?

- When do they want the candidate to start? (Some jobs have specific start dates for a group of hires while others are on a rolling basis.)

- When can you expect to hear back regarding the job?

Tailor your resume and practice interviewing.

I have on my desktop my full resume as one document several pages long, with multiple bullet points that describe what I've done at all the places I've worked. When I apply for a new job, I do a keyword search and tailor the resume to match as many keywords in the job description as possible, taking out anything unrelated and emphasizing the skills that the posting is looking for. This exercise is especially important if your resume gets scanned by automatic screening software, which many big companies use to filter through all the applications they receive. After I apply, I actively practice my interviewing skills.

Do research on the company. If you are invited to interview, look at the hiring manager's LinkedIn profile to learn about their background (yes, they might see that you looked at their page, but they are expecting you to do this!). As you practice saying your answers out loud, try not to be too scripted; you don't want to come across as having memorized your answers, but you do want to have a practiced repertoire of stories and anecdotes to draw upon when answering questions.

Do your due diligence as you interview.

Keep in mind that while the company is interviewing you, you are also interviewing the company. If you visit the office, note the overall vibe, how the offices and desks are arranged, how people dress, and what their personalities are like as they work. If an interviewer goes out of their way to be mean or indifferent during an interview, I take that as a sign of what kind of work environment to expect. Here are some of my best questions to ask to get a sense of a company's culture:

- For salaried roles where the hours are not apparent: Can you tell me about a typical day or week? How often do people work late, and until when do they work?

- Tell me about my potential boss's working style (assuming you're speaking to their peers or direct reports). What kind of work do they like to see most?

- What are some of the characteristics that the most successful people in this company have in common?

- What are some of the most critical initiatives that this company is working on? (Listen for similarities among interviewers, especially from other departments or roles. In a company where there is not enough cross-functional communication, you'll find that people will give you different answers.)

- If there is one thing you could improve about the company, what would it be? (This signals to me the most undesirable part of working at this company.)

Compensation Negotiations

Getting a job offer is hard. But once you get one, the most crucial next step? Negotiate that offer. This part can make or break how your income will evolve over time. Ideally, you want your total compensation to increase each time you change jobs. In reality, this can be difficult if you're switching industries, especially to a lower-profit one, moving to an area with a lower cost of living, or taking a demotion in responsibilities. It was eye-opening to see how leaving the fashion retail industry resulted in an immediate 40% increase in my base salary.

Knowing what kind of pay you can expect is a conversation to have both in networking as well as during your application process. Questions I ask when learning about a role include: What is the typical compensation band for someone with my experience? How high could it get? If the role is salaried, what is their budget for this position? For hourly positions, I would ask what hourly wage they offer for the role. Asking these questions also allows me to put the onus of the "What are your salary expectations?" from a recruiter back on them. When I get asked this, I answer with something like, "I'd be interested in learning about your budget for this role and its associated responsibilities. I'm excited to have this conversation to see if there could be a mutual fit." In the US, you are not legally obligated to disclose what your current pay is to a recruiter, so reflecting the question back to them gives you more power in a job search.

How much the company wishes to pay for the position has little to do with how good you might be for the job. Some companies are underfunded or simply less competitive than their peers. Some are completely guessing at the compensation because they've never hired for this role before. You hold significant power in a negotiation if from your networking, you know how competitive a job offer is. Don't be tempted to go for the first offer you receive because eagerness or desperation puts you in a weaker negotiating position. If you're not aware of how much it might pay, be sure to learn about it before you apply. It's like knowing the price of an investment, but it's your livelihood at stake! Additional considerations include the hazard level of the work, whether you would need to travel extensively, bring work home, or commute to and from work, the flexibility of your schedule, and how much time off you get. Roles that appear to be difficult should pay more.

Your pay is the total compensation—it's not just the amount on your paycheck. As a full-time employee, your benefits can be a significant part of your pay. The following is an inexhaustive list of things to consider when negotiating. Not all these items are meant to be negotiated; for some, you need to find out what the company offers and compare that against what you desire, i.e., put a price on what it means to you.

- Overtime, if you're hourly or nonexempt
- Merit bonus or end-of-year bonus target ranges
- Sign-on bonus and relocation assistance
- Number of public holidays observed
- Number of vacation days, personal days, and sick leave given
- Parental leave
- Health, vision, and dental insurance
- Short- and long-term disability coverage
- Retirement plan such as a 401(k) and what the company matches
- Employee stock purchasing plan
- Equity grants, restricted stock units (RSUs), and stock options
- Travel reimbursement

Compare all the parts of the job offer to what you currently have. Ensure you are compensated for any benefits you may be losing by switching to this new employer. For example, suppose one job offer has a 3% guaranteed salary match into retirement, and another does not, and all other parts of the two offers are identical. In that case, the offer that doesn't provide the match should pay at least 3% more elsewhere.

Once you've done your research, you will have your negotiations list. This includes what salary and benefits you'd like. Remember that some perks, such as healthcare coverage and the employer matching in your retirement plan, are determined at the corporate level and may not be able to be individually adjusted. Thus, you'd have to ask for remuneration in another way, such as a bonus or higher salary.

The actual negotiation can feel scary, and that's okay! Most of us want to be pleasant and keep the job offer. Self-advocating and asking for respect for your work shouldn't put your job offer at risk. Negotiating is simply an expected part of a job search, and the more you can keep your emotions from affecting the process, the better. I always begin with as much personal interaction as possible and prefer making a phone or video call rather than emailing. I start by thanking them for the offer because it is an exciting time! It could be the start of something great. I provide the elements where I would like to see an increase (always ask for a bit more than you expect because the company is likely to meet you in the middle). You may want to add some helpful context, though, again, don't feel pressured to reveal your current compensation, especially if it's a lot less. End with another thank-you. Then, you wait. The negotiation has been completed, the final offer should come in writing on company letterhead.

Let's be honest: Sometimes I shake from nervousness during a negotiation. However, a great employer will not take away a job offer because of what I'm asking for (if they did, it would be a huge red flag) and should be willing to make some concessions, especially in a strong economy. Turning down a job offer is also something you're allowed to do if it just doesn't work for you.

Job Promotions

If a job search is not in the cards for you for whatever reason, the other way to change your income is through a promotion or transfer within your current company. These moves, especially promotions, can be complex and require you to know how to manage company politics, especially as you step into more senior-level job titles. Getting promoted is often based on something other than merit, especially in corporate America. It's not how well you do; it's whom you know and how they perceive you. Company leaders like being around people they can respect and get along with. This means that upper leadership often appears culturally homogeneous.

The path to promotion differs for each company, but some aspects are the same. To earn a promotion, you want to embody the characteristics that lead to success at your employer. The key is to do something well that the company cares a lot about. One of my clients began working in his early thirties for one of the largest software companies in the world. He had started out with a lesser-known product line, but within that role he focused on what the company valued most and made sure that whenever he marketed a product, it led to above-average sales. As he moved through different products, he focused on driving more revenue, until eventually he reached the highest level of directorship that was available at his company. By his late forties, he was making well over $300,000.

Let's assume that you'd like to go for that promotion. You will need to have a few fact-finding conversations with your boss, peers, and other recently promoted people. Getting information allows you to navigate the process and create a concrete plan toward moving up. Essential questions to ask include:

- What are the responsibilities at the next level?
- What is the expected compensation change? Are there any changes in benefits?
- How long does it take a typical person at this company to get promoted?
- What must-haves do you need to prove to garner this promotion?
- How are you being measured? How often is the assessment happening? Who has the most say in your evaluation?
- Is extra work necessary to be promoted? Do you need to show the ability to perform at the next level?
- Are there any tests, classes, or certifications you need to take?
- What can detract from a promotion?

• Are there any specific skills that you need to have or show?

The purpose of these questions is to show that a promotion should be an ongoing conversation and not a surprise. This is especially important if you work in a smaller company where the process is not clearly defined. Asking about these procedures also helps alert your boss that you are interested and motivated in helping their company grow. Feel free to find time, in addition to formal assessments, to check in with your boss to see if you are on the right track so that you can course-correct if needed.

Finding a champion at work is helpful too. Mentors who are fully invested in getting you promoted are crucial. You develop these relationships over time usually by impressing someone more senior than you through your results. If they notice you, they may go out of their way to include you on other projects and initiatives and put in a good word for you as you are being considered for promotions. They can give you advice and help interpret your assessments and feedback, get you back on your feet in the case of a setback, and work with you to figure out the best next steps to take. Most of the corporate climbers I know had at least one champion who helped them navigate the company because so much of what it takes to succeed at a job is often unspoken and coded. Bing Chen, the CEO of Gold House, an influential nonprofit that promotes the Asian Pacific American community, spoke publicly of how he started the YouTube Creator program when he was a twenty-something-year-old, in the mid-2010s. Few people at YouTube and its parent company, Google (now known as Alphabet), believed in what he was doing, and he had to go to more than fifty teams to convince the organization to believe in this project.[41] However, once it became clear that his initiative was a profitable venture for YouTube, leaders started noticing him, mentoring him, and giving him more opportunities to succeed. These supporters were Chen's champions. He eventually became one of the fastest-rising employees under the age of thirty at YouTube.

Getting promoted can be rewarding because you get noticed for your efforts and receive a title bump and raise without having to go through the trouble of interviewing for a new job. It can also come with exciting benefits, like expanded responsibilities, more people to manage, and maybe even nicer company perks. As you move forward and upward, focus on your work. Keep a record of everything that you can celebrate! This includes copies of your deliverables and results, nice notes and emails, praise from people around you, and evidence of you delivering above expectations or ahead of time. If your boss manages many people, then they might need to remember what you did that was newsworthy. You want to come to a discussion about your career armed with these hard facts to show that the promotion is in your grasp. Most people will likely do some work at the next level before they are officially promoted, while some might manage projects before managing people. Others may need a year or two of upskilled labor before being recognized with a title change or more compensation. There is no set timeline for promotions; it varies at every level from company to company.

You'll probably spend more time on your career than anything else detailed in this book to increase your net worth. Most other hard work, including therapy, budgeting, and investing, doesn't take the same number of years as a career does. This is where it can be tough. Stay positive and know that you are progressing to your next big break, even in discomfort and struggle.

CHAPTER EIGHT

TAKING A RISK

Remember Esther in Chapter Three, who had more than $100,000 in cash? She isn't the only person I've encountered who sat on hundreds of thousands of dollars, too afraid to invest. As I took in more and more coaching clients over the years, I saw people refusing to invest even larger amounts, edging closer to half a million dollars. I assumed that the more money people had, the more likely they would be investing, yet this was not the case. I realized that it's not for lack of money that people avoid it. Rather, they have fear around the concept of risk. In this chapter, I will introduce you to why it is important to invest, explore some of the anxieties people feel, and give you helpful tips to keep in mind when investing. The advice will be helpful to both beginners as well as seasoned investors who could benefit from additional direction on what matters the most.

My Money Is Making Money

Growing up, I imagined investors to be Wall Street men who walked around the New York Stock Exchange in suits and ties, yelling at others while stock information flashed on big screens. There would be lots of "buy" and "sell" dialogue, and the people who made the most money got to splurge on nice steak dinners and bottle service at the end of the day. This picture might have been closer to the truth in the 1980s, when I was born, but it's not what it looks like today.

Let's start with the basics: What is investing? It means putting your money into something that will help you make more money. For most of you, this means passive investing, where managing your money is not your day job. You purchase an investment, then go about your day. After a few years, your money should ideally have grown in value on its own. Most people need to be investing in some form or another because of inflation. As the general price of goods and services rises, it is much tougher to secure your retirement if you just put your money away in the bank; the money sitting there will inevitably lose value over time. Thanks to inflation, the prices of products go up a little each year. Just think of your rent or your car, a carton of milk, or even a movie (when I was a kid, tickets were $5 at the local theater!). Yes, deflation—when prices on goods go down—can happen, but for the most part, inflation is expected to be the norm, assuming the world goes on as usual and the population continues to grow. Rising prices eat away at the buying power of your money. If you were to keep $1 in the bank for ten years, that $1 would not buy the same amount of stuff at the end of those ten years as it does today. For example, $1 from 1990 is equal to $0.43 in 2024.

Buying Power of $1 Over Time, 1990–2024[42]

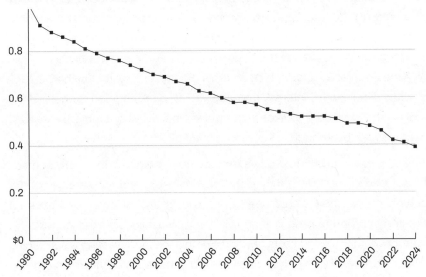

But if you were to invest that dollar in the US stock market, adjusted for inflation, that same $1 from 1990 would be worth more than $12 in 2024.

Value of $1 Invested Over Time, 1990–2024[43]

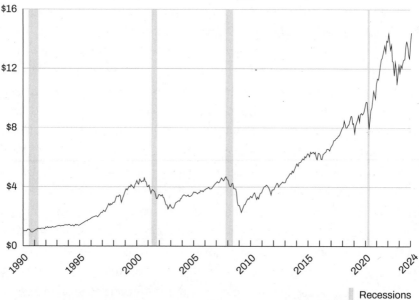

Recessions

What about the interest the bank pays on savings accounts, you may ask? Wouldn't it be enough for someone to save money in such an account to keep up with inflation? Well, the last time the US experienced high inflation was from 2021 to 2023, when the rates were 3.7%, 8.0%, and 4.1%, it was a while before the Federal Reserve, which controls the banking system in the US, took any action. For months, interest-rate payouts on banks lagged far behind the rate of inflation. Hence, if you keep your money in savings accounts, the interest earned may not be enough to keep up with inflation.

Let's say you plan to put away money in a bank to save toward retirement. For most people, assuming they work for forty years and then are retired for twenty-five years, they would need to save over 25% of every paycheck for the retirement fund to be sufficient. This is not a sustainable situation for most people, not with the rising costs of living. For this reason, investing is something you must do, even if your only goal is to afford a modest lifestyle in retirement.

Comparison of US Inflation Rate vs. Federal Reserve Interest Rate, Jan 2018–Sep 2023[44]

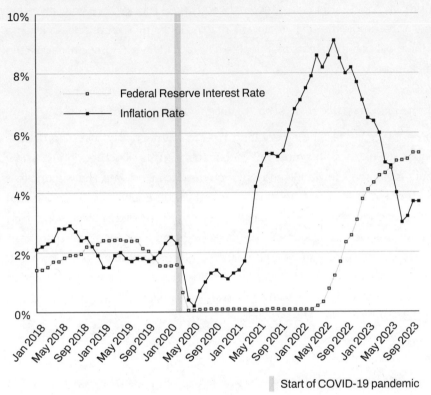

Start of COVID-19 pandemic

Your Top Investing Fears Debunked

If investing were a horror movie, it would be a blockbuster. Whenever I talk about the topic, the first emotion that my audience feels is fear. People get excited about cars, new jobs, sex, and relationships. Why do most people outside the finance world freeze like deer in headlights when investing becomes the main topic of conversation?

The media is partially to blame because it fixates on negative, shocking news. When I was ten years old and learned from my parents that we were moving to the United States from Europe, I was convinced that life in America would be straight out of a gritty New York City crime TV show, with robbers shooting guns in the streets and bombs going off everywhere. But just as our reality looks nothing like the *Fast and Furious* movies, everyday investing doesn't resemble the scary realm we imagine in our minds. Let's debunk some of the most common fears that people have about investing, specifically in the stock market.

"I've never learned about investing. I'm not going to be good at it."

Some things in life take a very long time to learn. Luckily, investing doesn't require a PhD, and the most basic concepts can be absorbed in just a few hours. As for the knowledge and logic you need to invest well, I have found that much of the reasoning takes shape around young adulthood. Teenagers can understand investing. Why? Because at its core, it is simply buying something that you believe can make money. If you know how a lemonade stand can make money, you can also learn how companies and markets make money. There are some great books to make investing simpler that I've recommended through the years, including *Broke Millennial Takes on Investing* by Erin Lowry and *The Simple Path to Wealth* by J. L. Collins.

"I need a lot of money to start investing."

People can become wealthy as a result of investing, but you don't need to be rich to start. As you can see from the chart below, if you start investing at age twenty and your investments see a 10% return every year, then it takes just $95 a month to get to $1 million. Two ingredients make for great investing: 1) time, and 2) investing in profitable assets. Because of time, a twenty-year-old doesn't need to put in a lot of money compared to a fifty-year-old. Time is the one element that none of us can reverse, but it is also the one ingredient that matters the most in investing. The more time your investment has to grow, the more it compounds and grows to a larger number. Part of why I was able to become work-optional in my thirties is because I started investing with my very first paycheck, when I was twenty-two years old. Even with relatively little knowledge, a few hundred dollars each month went a long way for me. And yes, you do need to choose investments that make money.

Monthly Investment Amounts to Reach $1 Million Net Worth by Age 65 (by age and annual return rate)

Age when you start	2% annual return (cash)	5% annual return	7% annual return	10% annual return
20	$1,143	$493	$264	$95
30	$1,646	$880	$555	$263
40	$2,572	$1,679	$1,234	$754
50	$4,768	$3,741	$3,155	$2,413

"It's too late for me to invest."

Some of you might wonder after seeing the above chart whether it's too late for you to begin investing. I would like to assure you: There is no such thing as too late. There's only starting later. Just as I want you not to define yourself by your debt, I also don't wish for you to define your financial journey by your age, as it creates feelings of regret that are counterproductive to your ultimate goal, which is to find financial peace. Of course, time is not something we can reverse, and that gives youth an advantage. However, many of my older coaching clients are also high earners relative to their youth and are able to set aside large amounts of money quickly to grow their retirement portfolio, making up for their lack of investing when younger. In general, as long as you have at least five years before you wish to retire fully, there is a high likelihood that your investments in the stock market will make money. Doing something now is better than doing nothing at all.

"I need to be good at math."

I've taught investing and retirement classes for nearly seven years to American students, most of whom don't use math to make a living. Many tools allow anyone with a high-school education in math to thrive as an investor. You just need to know how to use exponential math in addition to basic arithmetic; and if your math is rusty, there are calculators and software out there made for you, so you don't have to multiply exponents in your head.

Wealth is not just about math. If the best mathematicians were also the best investors, then the world's wealthiest people should be mathematicians. But most of the richest people in the world actually acquired their wealth either through business ownership (Bernard Arnault, Jeff Bezos, Elon Musk, Mark Zuckerberg), investing (Warren Buffett, Stephen Schwartzman of Blackstone, Ken Griffin of Citadel), inheritance (the Walton, Mars, and Getty families), or real estate (Lee Shau-kee and Li Ka-shing of Hong Kong). There's no denying that the wealthiest business owners in the world are highly intelligent and have a good understanding of finance to operate profitable companies, but you rarely hear about the winner of the Fields Medal (the Nobel Prize for mathematics) being mentioned as a wealthy person.

"I will lose all of my money if I invest."

As I mentioned in Chapter Five, the people I come across with the largest amounts of debt are usually those who bet everything on one company, usually one they owned. Herein lies the problem: putting all of your eggs in one basket. Mathematically speaking, the more diverse your investments are, the more you spread out your risk, and the less likely you will lose overall. Many of my coaching clients hold this belief of inevitably losing all their money if they invest, and it's often because they have seen or heard of failures. Several among them shared with me stories of how their fathers picked some stocks back in the 1980s that later lost a lot of value, leading their families to struggle and live from paycheck to paycheck. Those memories can have a very lasting impact and lead someone to avoid ending with the same result. But investing does not have to follow that pattern,

Imagine there are two people who each have $1,000 to invest. One person invests it all into a company that goes on to fail; they suffer a total loss. The other person divides their $1,000 equally into ten investments. Of these ten companies, one fails, seven remain healthy, and two grow. This person realizes $100 in profit by spreading out their risk.

Another way I temper my fear of losing my money is to examine periods in history when the world appeared to be approaching total disaster. What happened to people's investments during these eras? While we don't have records of markets in ancient times, we have over a hundred years of data for the US stock market via the Dow Jones Industrial Average. And if you look at the data, the line has never dipped to zero, despite depressions, recessions, world wars, crises, and political strife. This, to me, is reassuring because it means that there are always going to be ways to make money, in both good and bad times.

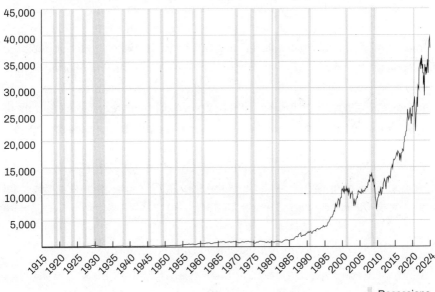

A Concentrated Portfolio	A Diversified Portfolio		
You invested $1,000 into a failing company.	$100 in failing company	$100 in healthy company	$100 in healthy company	$100 in healthy company
	$100 in healthy company	$100 in healthy company	$100 in healthy company
	$100 in healthy company	$200 in growing company	$200 in growing company
You have $0 at the end.	You could have more than $1,000 because some companies do better than others!		

The Dow Jones Industrial Average, 1915–2024[45]

Recessions

Yes, there have been recessions. Dips in the stock market are cyclical and unavoidable. Over time, businesses get inefficient, competition gets lazy, and a triggering event happens. The market realizes that there are stocks that aren't worth their current prices because the companies aren't actually doing well. So, the stock market corrects itself and pulls away from those companies, causing stock prices to drop. Underperforming companies either turn around their operations and remain on the stock, or they go bankrupt and get taken off the stock exchanges. When the market hits a local "bottom," it then starts a new cycle again. Eventually, investors gain confidence that the economy can grow again and return to the market. These ebbs and flows occur typically every ten years or so in modern times. Recessions are not a matter of if they will happen, but rather a question of when.

So, short of an alien invasion or a total implosion of the planet Earth, chances are there will still be money floating around. As long as you spread out your investments, you likely will be investing in something that is still needed during a downturn.

"I don't think I can increase my income enough to invest."

Some of you don't have enough money after expenses to invest right at this moment. You may be barely scraping by, living paycheck to paycheck, and some months you put expenditures on credit cards. Lowering your budget is the first solution, but increasing your income is the next step. As I mentioned before, there is only so much you can do to reduce your expenses; at some point, you can't lower the costs any further without potentially harming yourself. But there is much more income you could be making. Even negotiating or transferring your job can result in an immediate 10% to 20% bump to your earnings. According to a recent McKinsey study, over a thirty-year career, 6% of people who start out earning in the bottom 20% end up in the top 20%.[46] More income is possible! Let's keep your mind open to that thought.

"Investing in the stock market is just gambling my money away."

Casinos have some nerve! By design, they ensure that the "house" is more likely to win than the player will over time. Those with the Feast and Famine root cause often have the belief that investing is gambling, so from this perspective, it's no wonder the risk seems dangerous. However, while the casino can have a say in how the probabilities are designed into its games, the stock market does not have a single entity that controls it (that would be truly frightening if it did). Instead, it is subject to the world's randomness, such as geopolitical risk, natural disasters, and human activity. In that way, investing in the stock market is perhaps one of the most democratic ways for regular people to build wealth because rarely is anyone ever given a lasting edge.[47]

Think of investing in the stock market as showing faith that publicly traded companies are incentivized to be profitable. In most capitalist countries, that is the case. Corporations are manic about making money and could easily lay off employees during a downturn and do their best to outmaneuver their competitors. That's the energy publicly traded companies demonstrate. Because of this, the chances of someone making money in the stock market outweigh profiting from gambling.

"I need to know how to pick stocks."

Many people believe you can only make money by picking the right stocks (which I'll go into detail later). The reality is that very few expert traders are able to consistently make more money than someone who just follows the overall stock market. Many of my business-school classmates trained rigorously to become professional investors. They excelled in economics, capital-markets theory, and accounting. They brought their sample portfolios and theses to job interviews with investment firms and hedge funds. They went on to make a great deal of money, not necessarily because they were the world's best specialists, but because these firms charged their clients significant fees for their services.

You don't need to reach this level of investment to do well in the stock market. SPIVA (S&P Indices Versus Active) is a publicly available database that tracks the performance of professionally managed mutual funds and compares those against their index. In its 2023 scorecard, SPIVA found that over fifteen years, over 87% of actively managed stock funds in the US underperformed relative to the index.[48] That means that most of the time, even professional stock pickers don't necessarily beat the natural growth in the stock market! Now, this doesn't mean they are losing money; it just means that if all these fund managers had simply held a portfolio of all US stocks and didn't pick any stocks themselves, they would have made more money. Multiple academic studies looked at hundreds of portfolios of day traders—people who buy and sell stocks quickly, usually within a day, to make a profit—and found that, as a whole and over time, these traders didn't make as much money as a passive investor who bought and held their investments for the long term. Based on studies conducted in Taiwan and Brazil, less than 5% of day traders could beat overall market return.[49]

If you are new to investing, I recommend looking at robo-advisors or a software-based tool that helps you pick funds. This algorithm-based approach takes your input (such as your age, current net worth, and goals), then uses software to invest your money into a portfolio of funds, which may adjust over time. Because robo-advisors don't require the presence of a human person to manage your investments, it's also a lower-cost option for you to invest in the stock market. These solutions are provided by many of the top full-service brokerages (such as Fidelity, Vanguard, and Schwab, who all offer some form of automated investing advice) as well as companies that only focus on robo-advisors (such as Wealthfront, Betterment, and Ellevest in the United States). These are great ways for a novice investor to begin making investments without needing to read a stack of books about the stock market.

"I can't be the one to invest. I don't make the money!"

Many homemakers, particularly stay-at-home moms who are not actively earning income, have held this belief that they are not to touch the household investments. It is an outdated idea that the only person with the right to invest and make decisions about money is the one earning it. If that were the case, the economy would grind to a halt. Most researchers conclude that about 80% of consumer spending in the US (with similar stats worldwide) is driven by women, regardless of whether they are income earners. I think anyone who knows how to spend money can also learn how to invest it. The knowledge you need to make these kinds of decisions is more similar to developing a passion for a favorite brand or celebrity than your ability to have a career.

One of my greatest joys in running Save My Cents has been educating the nonearning spouse—especially if they're women—on the many ways they can assume the role of CFO of the household. It starts with learning about overseeing finances, preparing for retirement, and helping their earning spouse keep as much of the money being earned as possible. Interestingly, several studies comparing portfolios managed by women versus those operated by men found that women's portfolios outperform men's by 0.4%–1% a year, depending on the study.[50] Some of the reasons why researchers think this occurs include the idea that women are more focused on protecting their returns in the long term and don't react as quickly or emotionally to the market as men, despite the widely held belief that women are generally more "emotional." To put those returns in perspective, if a woman and a man were each to invest $10,000 a year for thirty years, and the woman got an 8% return while the man got a 7% return, this is what they'd end up having:

Person	Annual Investment	Annual return rate	Investment after 30 years
Woman	$10,000	8%	$1,130,000
Man	$10,000	7%	$945,000

That is a difference of over $188,000—a lot of money to give up just because you feel like you can't invest! I use this illustration primarily to encourage more women, who statistically earn less income over their lifetime compared to men and are less commonly featured in media, to feel confident as investors; but it is by no means meant to disparage men and their ability to invest.

"I didn't come from wealth, so I can't possibly become wealthy."

First-generation wealth builders—especially if you have the Scarce Immigrant root cause—have it hard. You didn't grow up around it. Other than what you can glean from media, you didn't see it in person often, so it's tough for you to imagine wealth happening to yourself. It's similar to how people who grew up all their lives in a small town have a hard time imagining what life in a big city might be like. If you are the first person in your family to be investing, you are not alone. If you will be the first multimillionaire in your family, you are not alone. Somewhere along the line, someone has to make a break for it and leave behind the mold they were born into. Your origin story doesn't have to define you.

"I can't invest while I have debt."

Hopefully you've already seen in Chapter Five that your debt doesn't have to define you or weigh your life down like a ball and chain. For many people, investing while you still carry debt is a good idea, especially if your debt has low interest rates. Think of the power of that extra dollar you have available. For example, let's say you have a debt with a 2% interest rate. If you put that extra dollar toward your debt, you are saving yourself from the need to pay 2% on that dollar for the remainder of your loan term. So, this year, that means you save yourself $0.02. Now let's say that within this year, the market grows 10%. If you put your extra dollar on the market instead of your debt, the dollar would generate $0.10 of value. That means you could spend $0.02 on the interest on your debt and still have $0.08 left to profit from! This is a simplified illustration, but it shows how not all debts must be rapidly paid down. My husband understood this concept better than I did, as he carried student-loan debt from his undergraduate studies that had a 4% interest rate. He invested while paying down those debts on time, benefiting from having his money grow more on the stock market.

So, for those of you with debt, I recommend you review the debt-free plan you have in place, realign it with the recommendations I made in Chapter Five, and see if you should be investing. You probably have an opportunity to invest earlier than you think!

Money Root Causes and Investing

The goal of sharing all of the investing fears is to help you feel that you are not alone. There is plenty of data and backup evidence that shows that the average person can be very successful at it as long as the focus is on diversified, low-cost investments. Before you start, there are some approaches I would suggest based on money problem root causes that may have been present in your life.

Investment Tips for Feast and Famine

People with the Feast and Famine root cause typically have the least experience of the three in evaluating risk. If you became used to making decisions quickly all your life, you probably didn't learn to slow down and think through the pros and cons of a major life decision. Deciding how to invest involves making calculated bets. I have met many coaching clients who were never taught how to invest while managing risk, and they often ended up investing in isolation and fear. They didn't know whom to talk to and didn't reach out for help. Another common thing I see with people with the Feast and Famine root cause is that they may get pulled in by too-good-to-be-true scams and high-fee investments promising instant wealth. By the time these coaching clients started working with me, they held significant investments concentrated in just a few stocks, which meant their portfolios were subject to more risk than someone holding smaller amounts in funds across hundreds or thousands of stocks. Furthermore, these people felt immense shame over not knowing how to invest or change their strategies. If you identify with this root cause, invest extra time in evaluating risk and consult trustworthy sources of advice. If someone pressures you to make a decision quickly, they don't have your best interests in mind.

Maria, the Feast and Famine person we've been following in the book, didn't even think of investing as an option for herself when we first started working together. She had only savings accounts for emergencies and for her daughter. When we first met, she had $19,000 in her employee-sponsored 401(k) plan. Using preselected funds instead of picking stocks, and with steady contributions from her paycheck, her investments grew to over $81,000 after three years. Her story is evidence that it doesn't take a lot of work to get started, and that even with no prior examples of investing in one's life, someone with a Feast and Famine root cause can easily guide their portfolios in the right direction with a modicum of education.

When it comes to investing, make sure that you are using fiduciary investment advisors. Typically, these are fee-only advisors who don't receive commissions and fees from the investments they recommend to you. Also, be hyperaware of your emotions as stock markets rise and fall. People with the Feast and Famine root cause can feel tempted to sell stocks when the market is not doing well. If you are investing for retirement, you should only sell your investments when you need the cash—when you are retirement age. Before that time comes, remember that recessions are an inevitability and downturns happen all the time, and hang in there.

Investment Tips for Adverse Events

People with the Adverse Events root cause often approach investing in an inconsistent manner due to the general uncertainty and volatility they exhibit in their personal finance behaviors. Mary and Bill's story shows how Adverse Events can negatively impact one person and cause them to behave differently toward investing. They are a married couple in their forties who approached me for coaching in early 2023. When we started working together, they had an impressive net worth of $736,000. However, I noticed something very interesting about their assets: They appeared lopsided. Their net worth included $145,000 in home equity, $160,000 in savings accounts, and $431,000 in retirement accounts. However, the vast majority of the retirement savings was under Bill's name. After verifying that Bill wasn't trying to abuse Mary financially, I asked why this came to be.

As it turns out, Mary felt anxious about investing in the stock market. When they made money from selling a prior home, she could not bear to transfer the profit toward stocks. She never felt smart enough or "good enough" to invest. She had tried once, at age twenty-four. She picked one poor-performing stock, lost money, felt ashamed, and then didn't invest for another twenty years. Bill, on the other hand, learned early on to put some money aside from his paycheck in a 401(k) and Roth IRA. Neither Bill nor Mary had parents who knew how to invest. What was the difference? Mary felt the Adverse Events root cause; Bill did not. For most of her life, Mary struggled with chronic illness, and her parents, who wanted to project a semblance of a perfect family life, hid Mary's disability. Her father, who was a perfectionist, would often "blow up" emotionally. Thus, she felt pressured all her life to be perfect. Her one experience with a bad stock pick convinced her that she could never be successful at investing. As for Bill, while his parents taught him very little about personal finance, they provided an emotionally secure childhood and made him feel he was loved for who he was. Bill had the emotional safety to not fear investing in the stock market.

Oftentimes, there is not much money available to invest when someone comes from Adverse Events. Instead, that money gets spent right away. If they do want to invest and have the money to do so, they may have a tendency to embrace the most risk possible and lay everything on the line. On the other hand, if you're using money to define your self-worth, you may be seeking hyperperfectionism and avoiding risk altogether, like Mary did. In this case, you are more likely to be overscrutinizing your every move and constantly questioning whether investing makes sense, perhaps to the point where you don't invest at all. For this group of people, I recommend that your investments be diversified and not concentrated in one business, one stock, or one home, as that is very risky. Read more resources that discuss how to manage risk so that you can gauge whether something might be too risky, or not risky enough, for your needs.

Investment Tips for Scarce Immigrant

People with the Scarce Immigrant root cause should be investing, but many of them avoid the risk. David describes his upbringing as "only having enough money for the necessities." His grandparents left the People's Republic of China for Taiwan during the Cultural Revolution, and David's father was the first of his siblings to immigrate to the United States by borrowing money from relatives to buy the plane ticket. David's mother also immigrated from China to the US under similar circumstances. When he was a child, his parents went on to higher education, secured advanced degrees, and became lifers at a longstanding Silicon Valley technology company. David told me, "My dad always had us question if any purchase was necessary. He always told us to avoid wasting items that could be reused, and don't ever put your money into the stock market," having seen how other people had lost money trading stocks. Combined with their immigrant mentality of needing to secure a future, they put all of their savings into paying down their mortgage and buying rental homes. Throughout his twenties and thirties, David did the same: He secured a good corporate job in technology, and outside of contributing enough to get his employer match in his 401(k), he used his extra savings to buy real estate.

By the time I worked with David and his wife, they had amassed a very impressive portfolio that consisted of $3 million in real estate (the home he lived in and a property he rented out) in Northern California and $1 million in index funds. When they shared their retirement goals with me, I noted that it would make more sense for them to invest more into the stock market with the hopes of higher returns than to pay down a mortgage with an interest rate of less than 3%. David was told by his parents to be very afraid of the stock market. He said, "Looking at stock prices is stressful. I didn't really contribute more to my 401(k) because I always thought the stock market was gambling. I didn't spend the time learning about how it could be pretty simple." It was not until his early forties that he finally began focusing on how to generate more returns in his portfolio to prepare for retirement and spend more time with his children. Before then, he'd been diligently making extra payments to get mortgage-free. Given the tremendous value of his two properties, David was not in a bad spot financially, but from an investing point of view, having so much of his wealth concentrated in just two homes actually created a blind spot for David. He admitted, "It did not occur to me that I could be making more money if I shifted more toward the stock market."

Many immigrants and their families come from places where an unstable government could seize banks, assets, real estate, and anything else of value. They may have witnessed hyperinflation, deflation, and financial disasters. Immigrants need reassurance there is no bogeyman waiting to grab all their money once they have "made it." Almost every Scarce Immigrant coaching client begins by telling me how their parents often have no experience investing, don't trust the stock market, and advise their children to park their savings ideally in a bank account or at least in a house where they can physically see their tangible assets. The conservatism of the Scarce Immigrant mentality leads to a strategy that might not adequately match their retirement goals. If you relate to this root cause, you need to recognize that some amount of risk is better than none, and it is also possible to avoid the extreme levels of risk our parents faced. Remember to diversify your holdings so that you are not putting them all in one kind of asset.

How to Start Investing

Once you decide investing is the way forward, you've taken a big step. Congratulations, you're on your way to wealth! But it can be overwhelming to know where to begin. I get it. To this day, I still feel butterflies in my stomach whenever I make a trade in my accounts. If you have already started investing, you may be wondering how to ensure there is adequate diversification, but also risk management, to ensure growth and enough protection when you need to access the money. We'll go through a few types of investments to consider first, then we'll look at some important elements that determine whether they are giving you good returns. I also recommend reading *The Bogleheads' Guide to Investing* by Taylor Larimore, Mel Lindauer, and Michael LeBoeuf. There are many more great books that go in depth on this journey.

Common Types of Investments

Stocks: Publicly traded companies issue stocks, or units of ownership in the company, so people can invest in them. Each company has a predetermined number of shares which is somewhat arbitrary; they can always change it. The stock price is, generally speaking, the company's total market value divided by the number of stocks. Being a shareholder gives you a right to a company's profits, which are paid out as dividends. The more shares you own, the more of the company you own, and the more you'll receive during earnings season. Most publicly traded companies get listed on at least one major stock exchange in the US, such as the New York Stock Exchange or Nasdaq.

Bonds: A bond is a form of debt that you can buy and is typically issued by governments and corporations, among others. Bonds pay out interest to buyers on a regular basis, and the bond itself can also be priced and traded. On the bond's maturity date, the debtor has to pay back the debt in full to the investor. In the US, lenders are prioritized over shareholders to be paid back in the event the underlying company goes bankrupt.[51] For this reason, investors have historically perceived bonds to be more stable and "safer" than stocks. You can buy bonds from the US Treasury website (treasurydirect.gov). Many financial institutions also offer more accessible ways to purchase multiple bonds through bond funds, or they may group bonds into mutual bond funds.

Mutual funds, ETFs, index funds, target-date funds: A mutual fund is a fund that a financial institution puts together for you to invest in and can contain various types of assets. For example, one might contain both bonds and stocks. Types of mutual funds include index funds and target-date funds. Mutual funds are priced once a day because the investments they contain change price throughout the day and then are averaged out to a closing price. Exchange-traded funds (ETFs) are similar to mutual funds in that they also contain various types of assets, but ETF prices vary throughout the day like a stock. In general, if you see both a mutual fund and ETF invest in the same set of stocks and bonds, you can generally assume that they would behave similarly.

An index fund is a fund that follows a stock index, which is like a temperature read, or "average," for a market. An index takes all the stocks that are in a particular market or exchange and averages out their price movements. For example, a fund that invests in US stocks typically tracks the S&P 500, which is an index of the five hundred largest companies traded in the United States. A professional fund that performs better than that index would be considered a high-performing fund; if it performs worse, then that index is underperforming.

A target-date fund is a fund that adjusts its holdings as you age and get closer to your retirement, or target, year. Many such funds start mostly with stocks and then blend in more bonds as the target year approaches. That is because a target-date fund's strategy is to lower risk as the investor approaches their retirement, and bonds help achieve that goal.

Real estate: Real estate is also something you can invest in, but it's traded very differently. Whereas stocks and bonds can be traded easily via computers, most people still buy and sell real-estate the old-fashioned way, with paper contracts that you execute in person via lawyers and agents. Real estate can consist of land, commercial buildings, or residential buildings. Most people in the US usually refer to buying a home to live in when they think of real estate. However, many people make money by being landlords—renting out houses and apartments to other people.

Measuring Performance

I'm going to put out some math equations here, but don't panic. If you have learned high-school math, these calculations are doable. Measuring the performance of your investments is crucial because that is the only way you can tell whether your investments are growing or not. You don't need to memorize these formulas and concepts; you can just bookmark these pages and come back at a later time.

Risk tolerance: What would happen if I told you to take all your investments and play a game of poker with it? Some of you might bet on every hand. Some of you might fold as soon as you think you have a losing set of cards. How you approach something like a game of poker is a great way of determining your risk tolerance, which is the amount of vulnerability or exposure that you are willing to take in your portfolio based on your individual needs and personality. Some people enjoy the uncertainty, and they tend to go into riskier bets such as individual stocks, day trading, options trading, or currency trading. The chances of making a lot of money are high, but so are the chances of losing a lot. Others are highly intolerant of risk and may choose to park the majority of their savings in US Treasury bonds for most of their lives. There would be little growth, but also little risk of losing money. Neither of these approaches is necessarily incorrect. It is important that you match your investing to your risk tolerance so your portfolio and your expectations for it are aligned.

Time horizon: The length of time before you need your investment returned to you as cash is called the time horizon, or investing horizon. For example, if you just had a child this year and want to save for their college tuition, then the time horizon, for their college fund is around eighteen years. If you are thirty-two today and wish to retire at age sixty-five, the time horizon for your retirement fund is thirty-three years. In general, the longer your time horizon, the more risk your investment can take on because there is more time for that investment to recover losses and grow. This is why younger investors and older investors often act differently when it comes to retirement

Annual return/Compound Annual Growth Rate (CAGR): You can evaluate how good an investment is by its annual return, which is how much an investment grows over the course of one year. The return in a given year is expressed as a percentage of the original amount you put in. To find the annual return of an investment, take the value of your investment at the end of the year and subtract it by the initial value when you first purchased it; then divide by the initial value. For example, suppose you invested $100, and that investment is now worth $110 at the end of one year. The annual return of your investment would be ($110 - $100) / $100 = 10%.

Annual Return Formula

$$\frac{\text{Value at the end of the year} \quad - \quad \text{Value at the beginning of the year}}{\text{Value at the beginning of the year}}$$

Looking at returns year to year might not give a clear picture of how your investments are performing. You could be up 10% one year, down 5% another year. How would you measure the performance of an investment that doesn't perform evenly across multiple years? The CAGR (pronounced "kagger") formula.

CAGR Formula

$$\left(\frac{\text{Final value}}{\text{Initial value}}\right)^{\left(\frac{1}{\#\ \text{of years}}\right)} - 1$$

For example, take an investment of $1,000 that grew to $4,000 over the span of ten years. What is the CAGR of this investment? It would be at 15% annual return each year.

CAGR Calculation of $1,000 Growing to $4,000 Over 10 Years

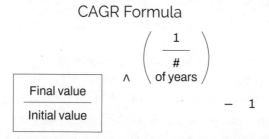

$$\left(\frac{4000}{1000}\right)^{\left(\frac{1}{10}\right)} - 1 = 15\%$$

CAGR is also referred to as compound interest. This means that as your money makes interest, that interest also generates interest; so instead of growing in a straight line on a chart, it grows like an ever-increasing curve. An investment of $1,000 that grows 15% a year would see increasing amounts of growth each year.

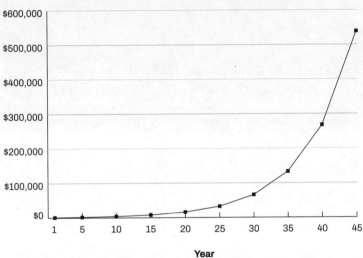

Annual Compounding Growth of 15% on an Initial $1,000 Amount Over 45 Years

As you can see, investing is not just growing what you have right now; it's growing what that initial investment will grow. It can compound and help secure your wealth for the future!

Net expense ratio: Just like banks can charge convenience fees or account fees when you bank with them, investments also have associated costs. Most of the time, mutual funds have to charge some fees to cover the costs of the fund managers who pick the stocks that go into the fund, the paperwork and reporting required by law, the technology used to provide the investment, and more. For most funds, this cost is known as the net expense ratio. Paying attention to this figure is very important as it could make or break the return on your investment. It is an annual fee that the fund charges, expressed as a percentage of the dollar amount you have invested in that fund. This fee is charged whether the fund grows or loses money in each year.

Let's say, for example, that you allocate $10,000 to a one-time investment. You have two funds to pick from: one charges a net expense ratio of 0.1%, and the second charges 0.5%. The table below shows the impact of the net expense ratio on your investment, assuming equal performance of 10% return a year over the course of thirty years. The higher the fee, the less your investment is worth. For this reason alone, and in conjunction with the SPIVA data presented earlier in this chapter, it is generally strongly recommended that you keep your investments in funds that charge low net expense ratios so that you can have the most growth.

Impact of Net Expense Ratio on a One-time $10,000 Investment Over 30 Years

Year	0.1% Net Expense Ratio	0.5% Net Expense Ratio
1	$10,990	$10,950
10	$25,703	$24,782
20	$66,062	$61,416
30	$169,797	$152,203

I once shared at a corporate presentation that I always feel butterflies in my stomach whenever I execute a trade. This feeling is normal. Investing in the stock market is not tangible, and you can't feel numbers on a screen. It can take years before you see consistent growth. "Invest at your own risk" is a phrase that you will hear in the financial world because tomorrow is unknown. It's okay not to know what tomorrow holds. In terms of your retirement, I recommend you review your investments every year to make sure that the portfolio matches your risk tolerance, your investment goals, as well as the time horizon you have for that money. Given the volatility of the stock market, I don't think it's necessary to check your holdings every day. Stay up to date on the economy by reading financial news through outlets such as *The Wall Street Journal* or the business section of the *New York Times*, and continue to use data to inform your decisions as you learn. You will never have perfect amounts of data, so, like me, you will always be investing and doing it scared. And that is okay.

CHAPTER NINE

VALUES-BASED SPENDING

In 2019, I was featured for the first time in a major news outlet, a *New York Post* article entitled, "Inside the Strange, Secretive Lives of Rich Millennial Cheapskates." For those who are unfamiliar with the *Post*, it's a media company that thrives on publishing articles that are not fully researched and often based on Reddit posts. Sometimes it reports local breaking news in New York City, which is why I read it. When I first spoke to the journalist, we spent the majority of our call talking about how meaningful it can be to have a life with financial freedom. However, the article focused on painting my lifestyle and that of others as "cheap," highlighting how we got used items and wore our clothing until it was threadbare. The tone was more like, *Oh look at these strange people*, instead of, *Here is how they are pursuing a life of freedom.* While I initially felt embarrassed by the low standard of journalism in this article, I eventually realized it was an opportunity. I could use this exposure to spark a broader conversation about how people perceive low-cost living.

The reality is, most Americans spend too much every year to afford future retirement. According to a 2023 report by LendingClub, 49% of people earning over $100,000 reported they were living paycheck to paycheck.[52] Fifty-five percent of Americans can't cover a $1,000 emergency from their cash savings alone.[53] These are sobering stats. One can't spend one's way toward wealth. I believe that most of you reading this book can get to a place where you can feel financially stable. In this chapter, I will show you the most impactful ways to live below your means by aligning your spending with your values. Then we will explore how to create a sustainable budget.

Boundaries and Social Media

Your family and friends and what you see on social media may feed your money problems. My top tip for those learning to cut their expenses may not be what you'd expect: I encourage people to start with their phones. Changing the people who influence my life and regulating the information I consume have had the most impact on my ability to forge a frugal life without feeling judged by others.

For some people, you may need to have little to no contact with them. This is especially true for people who experienced the Adverse Events root cause, where even the thought or presence of a specific person could set your mental health on a spiraling path. Your time and resources are limited. When I first embarked on my frugal journey, I struggled to relate to my college and business-school classmates. Many of the meals my friends wanted to eat cost more than $100 per person, and I received invites to weddings that involved flights to Hawai'i and overnight stays at the Four Seasons. These events were simply too expensive for the budget that my husband and I had agreed to. Most of my female classmates carried designer purses that cost more than $1,000, whereas I hesitated for two years before buying a large $350 Michael Kors bag. In the mid-2010s, the job market was robust for MBA graduates, and it was not uncommon for many of my classmates to take months off in between jobs and call it "funemployment," which I thought was a very insensitive phrase, given that unemployment was not a choice for most Americans. I often agonized over meeting my friends without busting my budget, and my angst showed publicly. One of my longest-standing friends from high school eventually noticed and reached out. She assured me that she didn't care how much we spent when we hung out together. I should find a restaurant that fits my budget, she told me, and she'd be happy to see me. Her honesty and gentleness stood out, and I realized that a true friend doesn't measure the value of our friendship based on how much I spend on them.

Setting relationship boundaries will be critical to your financial journey. I've seen many of my clients being taken advantage of by their close family and friends, and they can only move forward if these relationships change somehow. In one such instance, my client was the first person in her family to earn a college degree and make six figures. Her relatives expected her to send money home to support everyone else and provide lavish holiday gifts. However, she had over $100,000 of student-loan debt, and when she took into account how much she spent on the family, she found she had little money left over to pay her loans. When she realized that her family was negatively affecting her debt-free journey, she had to make a difficult decision to set boundaries on how much she would support her family financially. When considering if a relationship needs to change or end, say to yourself: "If they don't respect me and my boundaries, then they don't deserve my money and time."

Social media also creates immense pressure. Everyone presents an idealized version of their lives online and most tend not to show the times that are hard or unpleasant. When we see these perfectly edited versions of other people's lives, we may believe we must live similarly in order to belong. The fear of missing out is real. It's human to want acceptance from others; social media amplifies this psychological desire. But remember that it is also the output of billions of dollars in advertising money. In the tech world, which produces the platforms we all use, there's a common bit of wisdom that states, "If a product is free for you to use, then *you* are the product." We aren't using Facebook, TikTok, or Instagram because these services serve us. Rather, our attention, time, and eyeballs are being "purchased" for free and sold to the highest-bidding advertiser.

It takes skill and knowledge to detect the sinister side of social-media. On the surface, social media offers fun, entertainment, and even validation. However, a 2020 study of over 150,000 teenagers across twenty-nine countries found that social-media use results in lower levels of life satisfaction and less friend support, putting the teenagers at risk for psychological issues.[54] There's no way around it—using social media all the time has adverse effects on our mental health. However, it's relatively easy to limit its presence in your life. Consider doing any or all of the following:

- Set a timer on how long you will use each app.
- Avoid using your phone when you first wake up or when you are about to go to bed.
- Unfollow accounts that don't align with your values and goals.
- Temporarily mute or remove from your feed the friends you still wish to follow but whose content you don't want to see at the moment.
- Uninstall apps or use blockers on your computer when you need to concentrate.
- Move your phone physically away from you, such as in another room, when you don't need it.
- Delete or take time off from social media altogether.

By doing any or all of the above, you limit the negative impact social media has. Your mental health is likely to improve, which then improves your ability tocontrol your thoughts around spending and reduce your tendency to purchase things based on impulse and emotion.

Housing

Housing is typically the biggest expense in any budget. Having lived in Boston, Chicago, San Francisco, and New York City, I am no stranger to skyscraping rent and housing prices. I learned quickly that I did not need to have a place all to myself. I didn't like paying a lot for housing, and in the years when I worked long corporate hours, I wasn't spending much time at home anyway.

Roommates and housemates are crucial to bringing down housing costs. I lived with other people for most of my working years between graduation and getting married, though, of course, living with others comes with its share of conflicts. Luckily, none of my roommates were true troublemakers, and I wouldn't complain much anyway since I'm sure I wasn't a perfect roommate myself. Over the years, as I kept relocating, I started paring down my belongings because it was a burden to move them every time. By the time I left business school for San Francisco, everything I owned fit in ten boxes and suitcases that could be shipped via FedEx. I realized that housing could be pretty affordable if you didn't own a lot of stuff and didn't have kids.

Things became intense when I moved to New York City with my husband. Our first apartment together measured 420 square feet, with most of the space dedicated to a living room and a bedroom. There were three tiny closets, an oven range with a two-burner stove, a sink, and a fridge that came up to my eyebrows in height—and I'm five-foot-two. This apartment provided a natural limit to my spending because it couldn't fit much. I furnished it mostly with used furniture. This included the bed I carried up with the (one) man with a van, an IKEA coffee table from our business-school classmate that we also used as our dining-room table, two chairs my husband had, and a sleeper couch left behind by the previous tenants, who were friends of ours. The only brand-new furniture we bought was a card table and a sofa from Target. We put our bed on risers to use the thirty-square-foot area underneath to stow most of our belongings that didn't fit into the closet. I also stored items underneath my desk at work, including rolls of paper towels and toilet paper, snacks, and half my shoe collection. Everything that came into the house underwent scrutiny; it had to be lightweight, serve a purpose, and be in frequent use.

While I was never fully comfortable in this apartment, I don't regret living there. It allowed us to save thousands of dollars each month that otherwise would have gone into a place we wouldn't remember all too much anyway. Splitting our housing costs was the number one reason our costs were low. Here's how my Trigger, Action, Reward looked:

Trigger: Something breaks in the apartment, or I notice how small the place feels.

Action: I remind myself that I get to live in the heart of NYC, a dream for so many people, in an apartment with a comfortable level of temperature, safety, and convenience. I get to see the sunrise from our large windows, and I have friends who want to visit us in our space.

Reward: I see the richness in my life and feel encouraged to keep going, all while our savings pile up.

Here's the math: If my husband and I saved $2,000 a month in rent (relative to a market-rate apartment) for just two years, which means netting $48,000 by the time I turned thirty years old, then just the savings from those two years would grow to be worth $500,000 (assuming a 7% per year growth rate) by the time I turned sixty-five. In reality, it was because we both managed to find low-cost housing for over a decade that we were able to build the bulk of our wealth in our early years.

Transportation

Car ownership isn't my first choice by a long shot. I was a menace behind the wheel as a teenager; my first accident was backing into another car as I tried to get out of a snowdrift in my church's parking lot. Owning a car is also very expensive, and since I lived in big cities for most of my life, there was always enough public transportation as an alternative. Luckily, it turns out that avoiding car ownership pays off. Most American households have one car for each adult who drives. Most American families also finance their vehicles. My husband and I didn't own a car until 2022, when we moved to Southern California and purchased my parents' fourteen-year-old sedan. This alone saved us a lot of money.

Let's put some math behind the savings. I probably would have gone for a Toyota Corolla as my first car in 2007, which cost around $15,000, or about $300 in monthly payments. Since Toyotas tend to last quite some time, let's say I drove this car until 2022. Because I lived in expensive cities those years, let's assume $1 above the national average for gas prices. Most Americans drive about fourteen thousand miles a year on average, and the Corolla gets about twenty-six miles per gallon with city driving. Let's say parking starts at about $200 a month, which inflates by 2.5% a year. Using CarEdge data, I can also estimate annual repair costs. If I added together all the costs (annual total car cost) and subtracted the public transportation cost I would have to pay (annual cost of public transport), the resulting savings (annual total savings of using public transportation) is money that could be invested. The final column (invested value of not having a car) shows the worth of that investment, assuming a constant 7% annual return.

I was thirty-six in 2021, so if we now inflate that $193,429 invested value that I had at the end of that year all the way forward at 7% a year until I reach retirement at age sixty-five, it turns out to be a staggering $1.4 million.

Today, as a parent living in Southern California, an area built completely around car culture, it is much harder for me to avoid. But any reduction in car ownership can be significant in wealth building. For the last two years, my husband and I managed to get by on one car for the whole family, since both of us have the flexibility of working remotely. While avoiding car ownership can be impossible in many places in the United States, if you're able to do so, then I hope this illustrates the power of cutting out one significant expense for perhaps even a year or two.

Year	Car payment	Fuel cost	Parking	Repair	Insur-ance	Annual total car costs	Annual cost of public transport	Annual to-tal savings of using public transport	Invested value of not having a car
2007	$3,600	$2,046	$2,400	$148	$1,137	$23,360	$720	$8,611	$9,213.43
2008	$3,600	$2,299	$2,460	$171	$1,166	$23,726	$738	$8,958	$19,443.32
2009	$3,600	$1,804	$2,522	$208	$1,196	$23,358	$756	$8,572	$29,976.88
2010	$3,600	$2,041	$2,585	$267	$1,226	$23,748	$775	$8,943	$41,644.44
2011	$3,600	$2,450	$2,649	$316	$1,258	$24,303	795	$9,478	$54,701.07
2012	-	$2,498	$2,715	$393	$1,290	$20,927	$815	$6,082	$65,038.03
2013	-	$2,439	$2,783	$549	$1,323	$21,125	$835	$6,259	$76,288.34
2014	-	$2,353	$2,853	$611	$1,357	$21,204	$1,500	$5,674	$87,699.52
2015	-	$1,858	$2,924	$669	$1,392	$20,872	$1,538	$5,305	$99,514.89
2016	-	$1,691	$3,997	$755	$1,427	$20,900	$1,576	$5,294	$112,146.02
2017	-	$1,842	$3,072	$766	$1,464	$21,173	$1,615	$5,528	$125,911.61
2018	-	$2,003	$3,149	$858	$1,502	$21,541	$1,656	$5,856	$140,991.21
2019	-	$1,938	$3,228	$901	$1,540	$21,637	$1,697	$5,910	$157,184.29
2020	-	$1,707	$3,308	$946	$1,580	$21,570	$1,740	$5,801	$174,394.53
2021	-	$2,159	$3,391	$993	$1,620	$22,194	$1,783	$6,381	$193,429.37

Everyday Cooking

I've joked to people that I didn't even know how to boil water properly as a young adult. My first job fed me a lot because any time we pulled a late night and worked past eight, the company would cover our dinner, so I would eat half of my meal and save the rest for lunch the next day. At my tech job coming out of business school, lunch was included as an employee perk, so I would often have more than enough leftovers for dinner as well. It wasn't until I got married that I realized that so much of adult life involves meal planning, shopping for food, cooking, eating, and cleaning up after myself. With a pot, pan, and rice cooker, I set out to learn the basics. How to control the heat on my stove so as not to burn meat. How to boil pasta until it was al dente. My husband and I ate lots of my failed attempts at cooking, and many times we resorted to using frozen prepared meals from Trader Joe's when the results of my time in the kitchen were not quite edible. Slowly, my cooking got better over time.

You don't need to be a professional chef to cook for yourself; anyone can assemble a sandwich or a salad. To keep our two-person grocery budget to less than $400 per month, I designed our weekly menu using building blocks, not recipes, since following recipes took too much time and money for me. Each meal consisted of a combination of three building blocks: a starch, a protein, and a vegetable. As long as I had those three things, I met basic nutritional needs. Using this principle, I started playing with how many combinations I could make.

- *Starch:* Rice and pasta were my main starches, followed by bread, quinoa, couscous, and lentils.

- *Protein:* Neither my husband nor I eat pork and shellfish, so most of our protein comes from chicken, ground beef, beans, and tofu. In later years, we added more fish and more luxurious cuts of animal protein.

- *Vegetables:* To save time, I mostly prepped broccoli, green beans, spinach, or premade salads in two ways: steaming then pan frying them, or putting them into soups.

You don't have to spend hours cooking either. Most starches easily cook without hands-on preparation using a pot or rice cooker. You can pre-cook protein by roasting fish, stir frying chicken and ground beef, and sautéing beans and tofu in large batches. Depending on what else you have planned for the week, you can also pre-cook the protein in a specific sauce or flavoring or just keep things lightly seasoned with salt and pepper, and then divide the protein into the different dishes and sauce them separately. For vegetables, many of them, including my favorites—green beans, broccoli, and spinach—can be bought frozen. Simply put the vegetables into a pan and cover with a lid, which steams and cooks the vegetables. Then uncover the pan and add a dash of oil and seasoning, which crisps the veggies. Veggie scraps can be kept for vegetable soup. I would start with a soup base that I'm already familiar with (either chicken, tomato, or a spicy Asian base), then add everything I have left to cook. Easy!

By having these building blocks prepped, you'll have endless ways to put your meal together the day of! For cooking inspiration, I like Good Cheap Eats because it focuses on budget-friendly recipes. You don't have to follow every recipe to a T; if there's an ingredient I'd rarely use again, I just skip it. You can also play with flavors by using a sauce or garnish. Here are some combinations for different cuisines, with the sauce or garnish underlined.

American

- Pasta + ground beef topped with pasta sauce + sautéed spinach
- Rice + roasted salmon + side of veggies

Latin American

- Tortilla chips + ground beef topped with melted cheese + side of salsa
- Precooked chicken in tortilla soup (fire-roasted tomatoes + onions + tortilla) + side of salad

Chinese

- Grain base (rice, rice cakes, or noodles) topped with meal-prepped protein (chicken or beef) + stir-fried vegetables (mushrooms, bean sprouts, or peppers) + Chinese sauce
- Rice bowl topped with meal-prepped tofu or meat + sauteed vegetables + green onions and a dash of soy sauce

As for dessert, my husband and I simply ate fruits, like apples, oranges, grapes, and berries. Half the fruits were frozen to save money, which we blended into smoothies. We kept things simple for breakfast too, with low-fat yogurts topped with nuts and granola.

When you start cooking your own meals at home, you'll notice that grocery shopping comes with its own price tag. You might balk at my liberal use of frozen food, but I want to note that many vegetables and fruits are flash-frozen at peak ripeness, which maintains their nutritional integrity until you use them.[55] Fish, in general, also has to be shipped frozen, then thawed for display in grocery stores, so it is rarely "fresh" when you buy it. The only way you can guarantee that you're buying fresh fish is by buying it live, straight from a tank, as Asian grocers offer, or buying directly off the pier when fishermen bring in their catch.

I also don't go out of my way to buy food labeled organic and frequently get into discussions on whether organic and non-GMO food is worth the premium. This is a debate that we are lucky to have in a wealthy country such as the US. Having worked in the food industry, I know that much of the fuss around "organic" and other wholesome labels is simply marketing. Conventional farming and genetically modified foods were invented to sustain a growing world population on limited land, and ultimately our health and longevity depend on a combination of factors. Good food is only one such input. For people looking to save money here, I would suggest you follow what you believe is best for your household's medical and dietary needs.

I'll be honest, sometimes it gets tedious when I feel like I don't have much variation in my weekly menu. And when I'm particularly tired, overworked, or depressed, I lean back on getting takeout. Here's how I've used Trigger, Action, Reward over the years to help stick with a mostly cook-at-home mentality:

Trigger: I feel too tired to put together a meal.

Action: I slap together a salad or make an "adult Lunchables" (a few crackers, some cooked or cured meat, and cheese slices). This could mean I eat cereal for dinner on occasion.

Reward: I save money by not eating out and feel satisfaction.

Trigger: The food I eat feels monotonous and repetitive.

Action: I research a new low-cost recipe to try to vary things within my budget. I remind myself that I'm lucky not to go hungry, as many people worldwide are food-insecure.

Reward: I am reminded of the blessing of being able to feed myself daily and continue to expand my cooking repertoire.

By my estimate, relative to other people, I saved at least $200 a month on groceries using this method and being mindful of the ingredients I purchased. I kept this up for over ten years of my married life. Compounded over ten years and invested at a 7% growth rate a year, this resulted in over $34,000 of savings. Extrapolate that to age sixty-five? Over $215,000 of net worth! It literally pays to cook for yourself instead of going out to eat.

Eating Out

Dining at restaurants is fun. In recent years, I have certainly indulged in Michelin-starred restaurants, fancy nights with wine, and off-menu items for which I didn't ask for the price first. I also grew up in a culture where food is the primary way people express love for one another, and I always had good nutrition growing up. When I arrived in New York City, forcing myself to eat out less frequently was the most difficult values-based spending habit I had to conquer. Furthermore, most of my friends who visited NYC on vacation wanted to splurge on eating out. But I couldn't eat out every week without wrecking my budget, so I had to find a few solutions to this dilemma.

First, learning to cook well over the years helped alleviate some of my FOMO (fear of missing out) around food. If I ate something delicious, I would learn how to make it at home. If it was simple enough, I'd replicate the recipe and, over time, make it well enough that I wouldn't feel like I had to pay for it all the time by eating out.

The other part about dining at restaurants that I had to address was the socializing. This was actually how Trigger, Action, Reward got started in my life. For years, I had automatically equated eating out with quality time with my friends. Have something to celebrate? Friend in town? We eat out. I realized that what I loved about it, besides the food, was spending time with people. But I could do that without going to a restaurant. In this case, my trigger was loneliness or feeling like I hadn't caught up with a friend in a while. Whereas my original action would have been to go out, my new action became looking for alternative ways to see each other. It could be eating dessert at home, grabbing a coffee, meeting up in Central Park for a leisurely stroll, or going to a networking event. The reward was quality time spent with my friend, and I would often take a photo so I could remember the day. I kept many of these photos on my phone, and it helped me realize how lucky I was to have such great friends.

It's estimated that people in the state of New York spend about $300 per person a month dining out.[56] In our lowest budget years, my husband and I spent about $100 per person a month and kept this up for at least five years. Collectively, we saved, relative to the average, $400 a month, resulting in $28,000 of savings over five years at a 7% growth rate. That amount, extrapolated to age sixty-five for me, amounts to over $233,000 in net worth.

Fashion and Beauty

I'm someone who subscribed to *Vogue* for many years and applied for jobs at Condé Nast. I worked in the fashion world for a top-of-the-line lingerie brand. I wore a Vera Wang wedding dress on my husband's and my big day, and I always believed that I would look successful if only I could afford a designer handbag. However, I came to question all of these beliefs as I went along in my frugal journey.

In the early 2010s I came across a concept that fashion bloggers called a "capsule wardrobe." The idea is that, rather than having lots of clothes to pick and choose from, you have a closet of just a few high-quality items to mix and match and create multiple outfits. To cut back on my clothes spending, I decided to fashion thirty different outfits out of thirty pieces of clothing for thirty days. If you have ten tops, ten bottoms, and ten additional layers (like cardigans and sweaters), you could theoretically make 10 x 10 x 10 = 1,000 unique outfits. It doesn't quite work that way in real life, though, because not every piece matches all the others perfectly. Still, I was amazed when my thirty-day challenge worked, and I don't think my coworkers even realized that I was wearing the same jeans most of the time.

To make my capsule wardrobe, I slowly reduced my closet to a few high-quality staples, sticking primarily to neutral colors to make it easy to mix and match. My accent color was everything in the red family: reds, pinks, and purples.

My capsule wardrobe didn't include underwear, socks, tights, or lounge/workout clothes, and I also kept a handful of dresses for special occasions, like weddings. For shoes, I wore athletic sneakers and flats to commute to and from work and kept two pairs of comfortable heels I could walk around the office in, which I stored at my desk so they didn't get damaged. I donated everything else that didn't fit into this concept.

Aside from the high-quality staples, I quickly learned to buy secondhand clothing. Every season, I would go to the store to try on new styles and photograph myself wearing them, recording the name of the clothing item, the size that fit me, and even the care label if need be. Then I would go home and add search alerts and do image-based searches on websites like Poshmark and eBay. Since I was in Southern California, I also added TheRealReal and visited a local consignment store called Twice the Style. Over time, I found these gems on sale and bought them for nearly 75%–80% off their original retail prices. Most of the items I bought from these websites were barely used (likely overstock inventory or clothing worn once then discarded by a fashion blogger). For workpieces, if it was something I knew I'd wear every day, such as slacks, I'd take them to a local tailor to get them altered. Nothing looks more elegant than a piece of clothing that seems made to measure; the perfect fit trumps the perfect fabric or an innovative style every single time.

My Wardrobe Staples

- Three jackets (down, wool, and trench) for outerwear
- Three pairs each of jeans and slacks (gray and black)
- Three layering camisole tanks (white, gray, and black)
- Three work shirts (white, black, and pink)
- Three to five sweaters (pink, purple, and neutrals)
- Three to five shift dresses (black, patterned, and pink) with similar A-line, short-sleeve styles

---

To make room for your capsule wardrobe, take a look through your closet and do a fashion show. Consider getting rid of these items:

- Clothing you barely wear

- Clothing that doesn't fit and would be too costly to alter

- Clothing that is "onetime use" that you could borrow or rent, such as special-occasion dresses or ski boots if you're not a regular skier.

- Items that don't match anything else in your wardrobe

- Items you hold onto because of nostalgia

Once you have your wardrobe, you'll need to hold yourself off from adding unnecessarily to it. Whenever I found myself triggered to shop or buy a piece of clothing, my action was to remove myself from the temptation, which often included unfollowing a fashion influencer online. I also set an alert for the item and told myself to come back later because cooling down and walking away was often the cure to my shop-happy emotions. My reward was that I still managed to look professional and fashionable, but at a lower cost.

This meticulous editing of my wardrobe lasted from 2013 to 2020, and on average I spent about $500 a year on clothing. I then had a few years where I spent more liberally on clothing, closer to $1,000 yearly. So, I saved $500 a year for eight years. Again, doing the math, that amounts to about $40,000 in net worth by the time I'm sixty-five.

Other Great Ways to Save

I could go through every expense category, but in the interest of brevity, I'll summarize some other ways I have found savings throughout the years.

Travel: My husband and I did "travel hacking," which involves using a credit card and loyalty points/miles to reduce the cost of travel. We would wait until a reward credit card had a huge sign-up bonus, sign up, and then put a large, preplanned purchase on it. Many of the charities we donated to take credit cards, so that helped us accumulate points quickly. There are many online forums and websites that can help you learn more about travel hacking and how to get great redemptions with a few points. Since the rules of these rewards change constantly, it's best to keep up-to-date with a resource that stays in the know.

Energy at home: Not overheating your house in the winter and cooling only select rooms in the summer can result in significant utility savings. A smart thermostat is super helpful here. Furthermore, we often found well-insulated homes to live in, which helped conserve energy usage.

Household goods: I borrowed a lot of household items when we first set up our home to see which things I'd use every day and which I didn't. Later, I also discovered the magic of "buy nothing" communities—Facebook groups in which people within a local radius offer free items they no longer need. From these groups I have gotten everything from maternity and baby clothes to children's toys, books, furniture, dishware, and more.

Streaming media: With the disaggregation of media, it now costs as much as an old cable bundle to have live TV via Netflix, Amazon Prime, Hulu, Disney+... it all adds up. It wasn't until 2020, when the pandemic hit and there was very little to do outside our home, that my husband and I finally purchased a TV. We still don't keep it in the living room, preferring instead for all of us to default to a non-screen-related activity for entertainment most of the time, such as going to the park, visiting his parents, or seeing friends. This makes watching TV an intentional choice rather one of convenience. We sign up for one streaming platform, binge a specific show or movie, and then unsubscribe.

Work perks: A huge advantage to working for large corporations is that they offer many work perks. The largest from which we benefited was good healthcare and coverage of in-vitro fertilization, as it otherwise would have cost us over $60,000 of our own money to have children. Other benefits we've had include business travel (we could book on our own and get the loyalty points that came with it), dining out (we could pay on our credit cards to get the reward points), discounted movie tickets, free legal advice, partial reimbursement of a birth doula, relocation assistance, free gym classes, internet and phone plan coverage, fees for professional conferences (we would see nearby friends in our free time), work retreats (we could bring our spouse), corporate discounts, clothing sample sales, holiday parties, and more. Don't forget to explore your company's HR portal to see what perks you might be missing out on.

Root Causes and Values-based Spending

I don't think frugality will ever be entirely fashionable. In many respects, my economical, values-based life probably looks a little boring to a lot of people. It can feel frustrating, restricting, and isolating at first. That is why your values and personal goals must be at the forefront so that you feel like you are working toward something you care about. Among my coaching clients, I observed unique struggles related to the root causes. I've developed some easy-to-implement behavioral changes that work well with the personality traits and habits that we are trying to work with. Feel free to take what you can from all the suggestions in this chapter, including the ones grouped by root cause below, and apply them to your life. If it does not work out, that's okay! Your money is still yours at the end of the day, and you can choose to alter your spending in a way that feels comfortable to you.

Spending Tips for Feast and Famine

The key to controlling your impulse spending is to cool the itch. It is an emotional response that happens a lot more quickly than strategic thinking. I like implementing a spending pause of at least twenty-four hours before any major, non-emergency purchase. You can keep your item in the shopping cart or save it to an online list. Let your desire for the object cool down before asking yourself if it is a need-to-have or a nice-to-have. As for differentiating between what is essential and superfluous, as you learn to pare back and save, you'll see many areas of your life where you can go without. Thus, your definition of "need" will change over time.

Spending Tips for Adverse Events

Be very aware of your emotions when making a purchase. Often, you might be shopping to heal yourself. Or you might be buying an experience or trying to undergo a physical alteration to try to become that perfect idea of a human being in your head. However, you're chasing perfection, which does not exist. Behavioral analyst Kelsey Hunter noted that people from Adverse Events backgrounds are "predisposed to have obsessive thoughts and low self-esteem" because of their upbringings, which can influence their spending.

Remind yourself that no one is perfect, and you are enough, just the way you are. Examine the present relationships in your life. Are there toxic people you need to remove or set boundaries with? Are you following only positive influences on social media? Have you limited your time spent digesting the news? Are there other, nonmonetary ways you can invite more positivity, creativity, or genuine connection into your life? Minding your media habits and focusing on positive relationships can significantly improve your spending habits.

Spending Tips for Scarce Immigrant

You might have the opposite problem when it comes to spending: You know how to be frugal but are afraid to buy something of quality in order to save money in the long run. It's like shopping at Walmart versus Costco: You get low prices every day at Walmart, but things may fall apart quickly. Costco has a bit higher cost per item, but it is usually of higher quality and will last longer. Also, someone with a Scarce Immigrant root cause is much more likely to hoard things because they're afraid they will need them in an emergency. According to the Association for Behavioral and Cognitive Therapies, simply decluttering and cleaning a hoarder's home will not solve the hoarding itself.[57] They have to take the time and energy to learn psychologically to let things go. If you always buy in bulk because it feels like the cheapest price but end up throwing away half of it, you're still overspending. Identify areas in your life where you are accumulating. Those are the areas where you may want to raise the bar on the purchase itself by going for a smaller, higher quality, not having a large stash.

How to Budget

We're finally getting into the topic of budgeting, which, as I explained in the beginning, was what I shouldn't have started with my clients. Now that you may better understand how you think based on your money problem root cause, you can see where and how you prefer to spend your money. Having a values-driven system allows you to create a budget easily.

I like planning my finances on a monthly basis because many bills are monthly (rent, phone bill, and debt payments). For those of you who are not paid on a monthly basis, here are some easy calculations to get your pay aligned.

First, find out how often you are being paid in the image below. This image shows how many total paychecks you receive per year using your pay schedule. Then, use the mathematical calculations in the image below, to convert your paycheck to a monthly number.

What is the most important number in your budget? It should be your *wealth goal*—how much you wish to put toward debt, savings, and investments each month. It doesn't matter whether it is debt or investments; all is wealth.[58]

Budgeting by <u>month</u>, not paycheck

Paycheck frequency	How to convert each paycheck to a monthly number
Monthly	No extra math. Use as-is.
Twice a month	Multiply by 2
Every other week	Multiply by 26, then divide by 12
Weekly	Multiply by 52, then divide by 12

As for how much money to put toward that goal, don't get too stuck on this. Go for as high a number as you think you can achieve for now, and you can change it later on as you learn more about your own situation.

The most simplified way to think about your budget is this: Your take-home pay after taxes and deductions, minus your wealth goal for the month, is your spending budget.

For those of you who are already actively sending money from your paycheck toward an employer-sponsored retirement plan, that contribution counts towards your wealth goal, so we would adjust your formula using this:

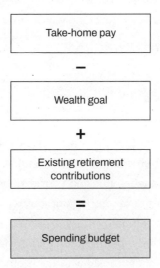

Now, let's make sure that your spending budget does not lead to debt. Add up all of your essential bills. This includes money for rent or mortgage, utilities, minimum debt payments, car costs (like gas and insurance), groceries, hygiene, healthcare, and care for your pets and children. Subtract that from your spending budget. What is left, if any, is what you can allocate toward nice-to-have expenses.

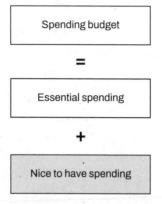

Spending budget

=

Essential spending

+

Nice to have spending

If, from this exercise, you end up with a negative number, then there are a few things to troubleshoot:

- Reduce your wealth goal.

- Reduce your "essential" bills (which might take some time, but changing your living situation can go a long way toward saving).

- Take a longer time to pay off debt.

- Make more income.

- Do some combination of the above.

If you prefer a little more detail, refer to page 212 of the appendix for more help with creating a budget. But that's basically it! The steps are not complex; it's the managing of emotions that is difficult. And here's what can help: Spend at least one hour a week tracking your expenses. You need to see the data and understand where you are in your journey at any given time. When you do so, don't beat yourself up over the expenses. Record them as neutrally as possible, and if you have a partner, don't fight with them when doing this. Instead, discuss your finances frankly with each other, hopefully every week. Approach each other with a willingness to understand and empathize, not to blame or raise a conflict.

There will be ups and downs! Every month is going to look different. For example, many people find their spending increases during the winter holidays and at the beginning of summer, when they plan vacations and camps for their kids. Got an emergency? Well, that can certainly skew your numbers. Added a new member or puppy to the family? You will be spending more. Instead of going for perfect months, pay attention to your average. I track using what I call the "trailing twelve-month average." In any given category or even in my overall budget, I average out my spending over the last twelve months. This smooths out seasonal changes, and then I compare that average year over year.

If you're having trouble keeping track of the numbers, use a tool that fits your lifestyle. Some people like using apps that connect to their financial institutions (youneedabudget.com is my favorite recommendation). Other people find that if they record a little each day, then it doesn't get overwhelming. And if you feel there are too many expense categories, then just simplify. You don't need many categories to detect how your spending changes. Some people go as simple as "bills" and "everything else."

Once you get into the practice of this, it becomes easier. You will be set up to achieve wealth. Remember, the goal of values-based spending might not be to spend the least on everything. It isn't always possible. However, most people feel satisfied and fulfilled knowing their spending is mindful and purposeful.

CHAPTER TEN

THE SIDE HUSTLE

Nearly fainting from the summer heat. Almost falling into a baptismal pool. Peeing my pants laughing at a priest's jokes. Almost injuring my back lifting forty pounds of equipment. Having a cold, sad sandwich for dinner. Sitting in a limo while crying over a breakup. Lounging poolside in Jamaica while enjoying jerk chicken. These are just some of the many memories I gathered during my ten-year span as a wedding and lifestyle photographer, a side hustle from which I profited around $200,000. Because I invested everything I made from it, I credit this freelance job, this mad passion of mine, which never made rational sense to me then, as one of the critical cornerstones that propelled me to build wealth early.

I never thought I would become a wedding photographer. My fascination with cameras started in high school, when I found my parents' old Nikon film camera in the back of their closet. I loved the idea that you could control every part of the creation of an image. I signed up to work on my high-school yearbook, thinking that if I were on staff, I could get more photos of my nerdy friends and me featured. Two years later, it became an all-consuming extracurricular when I became the editor-in-chief. I spent hours after school manually cropping photographs with grease pens and crop rulers to be sent to a service that would scan them for us. When the photos returned on a disc, I laid the book out in Adobe InDesign. We had a large staff of photographers and writers, but most gave half effort, dropped off their submissions, and left me with the grunt work. I edited and refined the copy, sent out rolls of film to CVS, and identified faces in each photograph, which meant getting acquainted with over a thousand student names. (God forbid someone's name got misspelled in the yearbook, as I'd never hear the end of it.) The hours were worth it, as our senior-year yearbook design won a statewide competition and a five-day journalism camp trip to the Columbia University School of Journalism.

In college, I took photos for many of my friends during their dance performances. For two of my electives, I took photography classes that taught me everything from darkroom development to post-production editing in Photoshop. Later, I tried my hand at photographing friends who'd gotten engaged, mostly directing them to emulate poses I'd seen on the internet. It was a change of pace from the tedious work I did in management consulting. As a beginning associate at a consulting firm, most of my tasks involved calling people on the phone, taking notes, doing a lot of Googling, sifting and cleaning data, and moving text boxes around in Microsoft PowerPoint. As I went about my job, I asked myself, What is it like to actually... do business? Somehow, the answer for me became, Well, Shang, start your own company and find out!

This chapter will give you some general advice around the dos and don'ts of starting a side hustle, with ideas specific to each root cause. My favorite book for further reading on this topic is Tim Ferriss's *The 4-Hour Work Week*. There are also many business coaches you can find online who will teach you how to start your own mini-business, but I would proceed cautiously and not spend too much money on them in your first year.

Overcoming Imposter Syndrome

My first photography clients were friends and friends of friends. When I ran out of friends willing to pay to be photographed, I began advertising on Craigslist. Within a few months, I booked my first wedding gig. I was a nervous wreck.

To seem professional, I borrowed additional equipment for the occasion. This was the wedding where I nearly tripped backward into a baptismal pool as the bride and groom walked down the aisle. But I kept going and made it through. After a couple years improving my photography skills and my ability to manage a fledgling business, I began to be nationally recognized. People wanted to book me for destination photoshoots. My work even got published in a few print magazines, which felt like a dream. At the height of juggling my consulting day job and my weekend job, I was averaging ninety-hour work weeks. If it weren't for the fact that I was still young, my body would have given out after a few years of doing this. I used Trigger, Action, Reward to get me through many doubts and challenges as an upstart business operator. Here are just some of the many situations I had to power through, mainly on my own.

Trigger: Imposter syndrome. I couldn't help but feel I didn't deserve to be called a wedding photographer. I lacked the training and experience of other high-profile photographers. I was "just" a businesswoman who happened to know how to operate a camera.

Action: I got to know my competitors and befriended them so I wouldn't resent them. I doubled down on my strengths—leaning on my sales background, being efficient and quick, connecting with people emotionally, and making them feel more confident on camera—and took classes in areas where I had room for improvement.

Reward: I realized that my competitors were just as human as I was and that I was, in fact, capable of delivering quality photographs to my clients.

Trigger: I was terrified of raising my prices.

Action: I asked for help and received excellent advice from someone to raise my prices by a few hundred dollars each; no one objected to the pricing. The gradual rate increases and affirmation when I successfully booked clients felt better than suddenly raising prices to what I "should" charge based on the market.

Reward: At the height of my business, my minimum fee for photographing a wedding increased from $2,000 to $4,500 (equivalent to about $5,800 in 2024). I'd found my confidence.

<u>Trigger</u>: I was emotionally dreading the sales process, as I feared not being able to win every client who inquired.

<u>Action</u>: I tracked my "booking rate," the percentage of inquiries converted into bookings. I told myself to see each no as more information for how I could improve my next pitch.

<u>Reward</u>: I felt better when I saw that my booking rate (around 33%) was good and steady! I stopped taking things personally and being deeply offended by rejections and evolved my sales pitches and presentations.

Root Causes and Side-hustling Behaviors

Not everyone has to have a side hustle to succeed financially. However, your money root causes can also influence what kind of freelance business makes the most sense for you.

Tips for Feast and Famine

For people who've experienced Feast and Famine, I strongly recommend that you work through an agency or marketplace (such as Upwork or Taskrabbit). Going through a third party removes much of the need to market yourself and put in too much of your own money to get the business off the ground. By using an agency, you're paying an established company to buy ads, find buyers for your services, help you develop a list of clients, process payments, resolve conflicts, and more.

I also suggest your side hustle employ a skill at which you are already proficient. Are you a teacher? Consider tutoring and babysitting. Have experience in finance or accounting? Consider doing bookkeeping or managing finances for a startup. Work in HR? Consider offering resume-review and job-coaching services. Don't do something you have never done before. You don't have the time to chase after multiple jobs only to find out they're not a good fit. Don't become someone who goes into hundreds of thousands of dollars of debt to support a failing business. Since Feast and Famine often leads to behaviors involving consumer debt, I wouldn't want you to start a side hustle using debt as well.

Tips for Adverse Events

People with the Adverse Events root cause often want to use aspects of their own experiences to determine what side hustle to pursue, rather than looking at what people are demanding or looking to buy. For example, I once worked with a part-time employee at a funeral home who had suffered an unexpected loss and thus felt called to work there. However, this person communicated unclearly, made multiple clerical mistakes, was not friendly to work with, and took a long time to return inquiries. She had few of the skills that would make for great customer service, and the position was not a good fit for her.

Don't let the side hustle consume your mind, body, and soul. Don't take the triumphs and failures of each day personally, which can hurt your business. Sammie, my client who was abused first by her father and then by an ex-boyfriend, learned that the market rate for a twelve-week program she was offering as a wellness coach was $5,000. She didn't think that she deserved to charge that amount of money because she herself did not have that kind of spending power. This is an example of someone taking numbers personally. Remember that a company needs to make a profit.

Tips for Scarce Immigrant

Those with the Scarce Immigrant root cause probably had their parents tell them to avoid starting a business. Due to the significant risk that immigrant parents have taken to establish themselves in new countries, often having to operate mom-and-pop shops to survive, running a business seems to be the last thing they want their children to do. Instead, they usually encourage their children toward more "stable" professions.

Scarce Immigrants also tend to do everything themselves and don't outsource or hire. After all, if you saw your parents do it all while managing to raise you to adulthood, why would you pay other people to do your hard work for you? The reality is that when you don't hire help, you can't scale. I've tried doing everything on my own too. In running my wedding photography company, I hired very little outside help. And I got pretty burned out. With Save My Cents, I learned from my past and invested more toward hiring help and buying software that supported my business. These changes meant that my work hours were much more sustainable and gave me the room to think more strategically as a business owner.

The Hustle Is Not for Everyone

You don't have to work ninety-hour weeks to make it financially. Even when I did so, it came at tremendous personal cost—missed reunions and weddings, the ending of my first relationship, neglected friendships, and the decline of my physical health. If you are a working person with many responsibilities, such as caring for children or older adults, a side hustle might not be in the cards for you right now. If you do decide to pursue it, recognize that you will need to make significant sacrifices.

Running a business can also take a significant mental toll. As much as I tried not to let the revenue I was generating define my sense of self-worth, the numbers did get to me emotionally. There will be tough years. You will encounter competitors who maneuver more quickly, who are better funded, and who have a better product and service. Luck is not always going to be on your side. If you have yet to resolve the emotions around your money and your root causes, those emotions will carry over to your side hustle. That can then further compound and make your money problems worse. Sometimes, the extra money is not worth it.

Making Your Hustle Profitable

I'm not here to tell you whether or not to pursue the side hustle you have in mind. Instead, I will give you the tools to determine whether it is profitable and worth the time, energy, and resources you put into it. We will first determine your hourly rate after taxes at your current job. Then we will calculate your hourly rate after taxes at your side business. Comparing the two will allow you to make the right decision.

Let's start by calculating your after-tax hourly rate at your current job. We do so by taking your take-home pay (taxes are removed) and adding back the money you put into retirement and benefits. Then divide that number by the hours you worked.

Now, let's estimate your after-tax hourly rate for your side hustle. You can do this across your entire business or by the product or service offered,

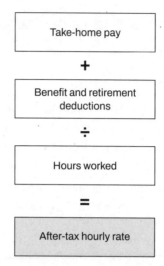

if you have very different offerings. (For example, my business is structured to offer two products: a coaching service, and a class.) Take your total sales and subtract your operating expenses. Then multiply it by 1 minus your estimated tax rate, so you can see what your profit might look like after-tax. Then divide it by your total hours worked to calculate your after-tax hourly rate.

If you're unsure of your estimated tax rate, I've found that 33% is a good starting point in the United States to account for federal income tax and self-employment taxes.

Once you complete these calculations, you can see how your side earnings compare to your full-time income. What if you find out your freelance work makes significantly less money than your day job? Here are some actions you might consider:

- Grow your customer and prospect list to have more people to market to.

- Improve how many of your prospects you convert to paying clients by investing in your marketing.

- Raise your prices.

- Lower your costs.

- Work more quickly and efficiently.

- Add more value to what you already offer.

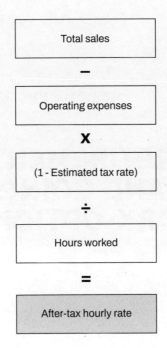

Maybe there isn't much more you can do to increase your profits. Maybe you chose a side hustle that is less profitable than your day job. That's acceptable as long as you're okay with it. If you grow your business and decide one day to take it full-time, spend energy on learning about business operations. Borrow books from the library, consume online resources, join a local business-owner meetup, and attend your industry's big conventions to expand your network and acumen. Also, discuss your decision to go full-time with stakeholders in your life—particularly partners with whom you share finances. Know that this transition in your career can lead to several months of uncertain cash flow.

I want to end by sharing an encouraging point: Many business owners and successful entrepreneurs got to where they are today by pursuing a passion project or idea. Many of my coaching clients who are reaching a multimillion-dollar net worth do so because they derive profits from being business owners. A side hustle can become your main gig, and it can also become very lucrative. Even if you don't take it full-time, the extra income can be the perfect way to turbocharge your ascent to financial independence.

CHAPTER ELEVEN

RETIREMENT AND GOING WORK-OPTIONAL

In 2016, I reached early retirement, also known as FIRE (Financial Independence, Retire Early). In this world, I define my status as "lean FIRE," which means a net worth roughly equal to twenty-five times my annual expenses, but nothing extra or luxurious. There were many good reasons for me to keep working. While it was a satisfying accomplishment, it still meant that if anything were to happen to my husband and me, we would need to make more money; moreover, we couldn't afford to have a child. And perhaps more than I'd like to admit, I wasn't sure if my feat was real. It wasn't until seven years later that I finally quit my corporate job to pursue Save My Cents full-time.

How did I reach the ability to retire at age thirty-one? Most people who pursue this endeavor use the 4% Rule, when your net worth equals twenty-five years' worth of expenses. I achieved the goal amount because I made as much money as possible, spent as little of it as possible, and invested the savings. For my investments, I focused primarily on low-cost index funds that tracked the United States stock market. The money I invested from 2007 to 2016 (the years leading up to my thirty-first birthday) achieved an annualized return rate through 2024 of 7%–11%. I didn't focus on real estate because I had no interest in it, though it is an excellent way for many people to build wealth. Now, you may be wondering how one can retire early when most of one's net worth is tied up in various accounts that do not allow access until age 59.5 in the US. Well, there are ways around this.

What follows in this chapter is a quick summary of the different accounts available in the US to save for retirement. I will how taxes are calculated, the main platforms you can use, an easy-to-remember framework to reference for yourself, and how early retirement works. There are more details in the appendix. For in-depth research, you can visit IRS.gov and various resource websites, such as Investopedia.com, and purchase my course. To be clear, the information shared in this first half of the chapter is relevant only to American citizens or people authorized to work in the United States. In the latter half of this chapter, I'll summarize the key actions you can take upon finishing this book, and then we'll revisit some of the coaching clients we have already met and find out how their financial journey has developed.

What the Tax?

You may be a little confused about why I'm beginning by discussing taxes because they might not seem all that relevant, especially if you're just starting to work. The way that the United States tax system works is that as you make more money, the percent of each additional dollar you make that goes toward taxes increases. That means taxes do not feel all that bad when you're early in a career and making less money. Only when you make more money and get taxed at higher rates will you feel the pain, and thinking about how to manage your taxes in the most efficient way possible will start to make more sense. I don't want you to miss out on several opportunities to save on taxes early on in life, so let's address that now.

There are three key ways that the government levies taxes that are relevant to a discussion of retirement. The list below is not exhaustive but gives an overview.

Income tax

When you earn money (e.g., working for another employer or your own company), the government taxes that amount using **ordinary income tax—** a tax rate that increases according to the amount of money you make.

Income tax on interest and dividend income

When you make income from your assets in the form of interest paid to you by a bank or dividends provided by your stocks, the government taxes that income using ordinary **income tax rates**.

Capital gains tax

When you sell an investment that you've held for more than a year, the profits from this sale are called **capital gains**. The government taxes capital gains at different rates from ordinary income taxes, called **capital gains tax**.

We almost always pay these taxes if we invest using a trading account, also known as a taxable brokerage. However, the US government created exceptions that allow people to save on their taxes. They are very important to learn because if you manage your taxes right, they may make a difference of hundreds of thousands of dollars in your final net worth at retirement.

The US government created three tax statuses to which your money can belong: after tax, traditional or tax-deferred, and Roth. The names are not intuitive but are essential to understand. These three statuses are not types of accounts, which I'll explain later; rather, they're ways that your money is characterized, kind of like flavors of ice cream. An account may contain one, two, or all three types of tax characterizations. Bear with me; it gets a little easier as we go.

After tax: If your money is after tax, that means there are no tax benefits available. You pay income taxes on that money first, before you invest what is left. As your investment grows, it can be subject to taxes on interest and dividends. When you sell the investment and withdraw the money, you may also owe additional capital gains tax. For most people, after-tax money is the state in which their money starts—it has already been taxed, and now they can spend after-tax money on something.

After tax characterization

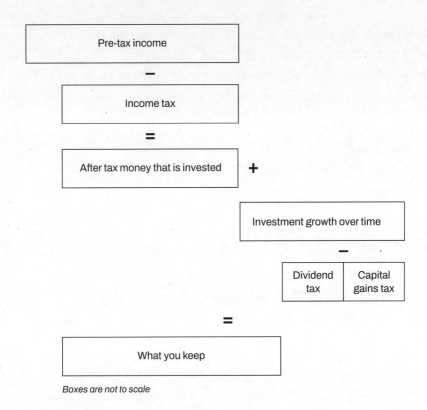

Boxes are not to scale

Throughout the late twentieth century, as more companies moved away from providing pensions for their employees, the US government decided to allow Americans to save for retirement on their own. To incentivize Americans to do so, the government had to provide some kind of tax benefit through these accounts. The benefits have evolved over time to be either traditional/tax-deferred or Roth.

Traditional/tax-deferred: This is also called pre-tax income. For traditional/tax-deferred money, you don't pay any taxes when you get paid. Then let's say you put it into an investment. That investment grows tax-free, so you don't pay any income taxes on dividends and interest. But when you withdraw the money at retirement by selling it, you then pay income tax.

Roth: Money characterized as Roth is taxed when you get paid. After you pay taxes and invest that money, it grows tax-free. When you sell the investment and withdraw at retirement, you don't owe any income taxes.

Roth tax characterization

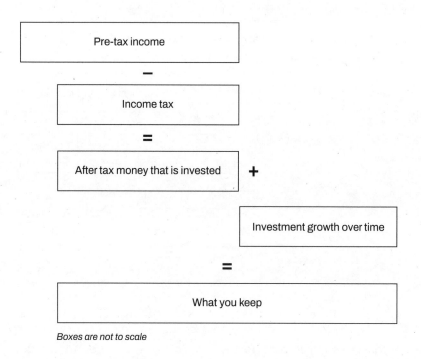

Boxes are not to scale

Now, let's take the above tax characterizations and understand the overall context of where they fit in the financial world. Words like "Roth" and "401(k)" by themselves are not investments, but ways to describe an account and how it works tax-wise. It can be really easy to get the terms mixed up. Let's start from the inside and work outward. When you invest, you can buy something as simple as a single stock (see Chapter Eight). You could also invest in an index fund, which is a fund made up of many stocks. Both stocks and index funds are investments that you can hold inside some kind of account, such as a 401(k), IRA, or taxable brokerage (I'll explain more about these later). The money in these accounts could have one or more tax characterizations, like after-tax, traditional, or Roth. You can open and manage these accounts with a number of brokerages or financial institutions.

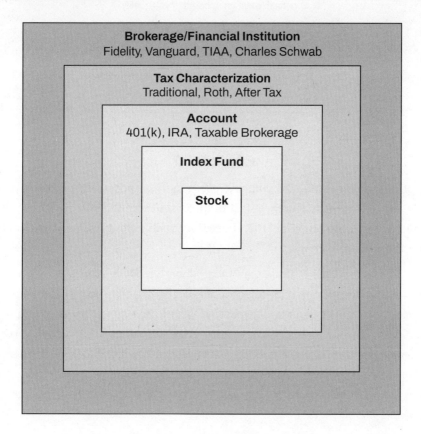

Financially savvy people understand that if you save your money as traditional or Roth, instead of after-tax, you could save upward of 40% on taxes. Your tax savings, compounded over time, could be more than $100,000. Now, the government limits how much of our money can be tax-advantaged, so I advise maximizing those amounts before keeping the rest as after-tax income. However, it's tough to keep track of all of this, so I created a straightforward framework to help people remember what accounts to use. This framework is called FHIT, pronounced "fit."

F	401(k), 403(b), 457(b), TSP, Simple IRA, Solo 401(k), SEP IRA
H	Health Savings Account (if you qualify)
I	IRA, or Backdoor Roth/Megabackdoor Roth
T	Taxable brokerage

F for 401(k)

If you are employed by a company, you may have access to an employer-sponsored retirement account. Most of these start with the number four (as in 401(k)) and thus form the F of FHIT. These F accounts help you save on taxes and invest for your retirement.

It is essential to understand that when we begin working, most of us will not have any money in these accounts. Most of the time, you must manually indicate to your HR department that you wish to opt in and begin saving for retirement. Usually, your employer provides these instructions on your first day of employment. The process is often electronic: You log into your company portal, select your wish to participate, and set the amount you want deducted from your paycheck. Here are the names of the different employer-sponsored accounts in a nutshell.

I like starting with these accounts for a few reasons. For one, you don't get emotionally attached to money already removed from your paycheck. Money is psychological, and these deductions don't make you feel like you're losing money. Also, these accounts offer a tax benefit of some kind (either traditional or Roth). Lastly, they are designed with retirement in mind—they make it a little harder for you to withdraw money before age 59.5 (and that's a good thing).

401(k) plans	Available to employees of for-profit companies
403(b) plans	Available to employees of tax-exempt 501(c)(3) organizations
457(b) plans	Available to employees of state or local government, and some tax-exempt 501(c)(3) organizations
TSP	Thrift Savings Plans, which are the 401(k) equivalent for employees of the federal government
SIMPLE IRA	Similar to a 401(k), typically available to employees of companies with fewer than 100 employees
Solo 401(k) and SEP IRA	Available to single-owner businesses with only themselves as full-time employees

Once you determine how much of your paycheck toward your retirement plan, the change usually takes about one or two payrolls to go into effect. Then the money transfer is automatic. But you still have one more important thing to do: select investments. Your employer-sponsored account's default "investment" is cash, but it isn't very obviously labeled. It could be named something like government funds, treasury funds, money-market funds, stable funds, or core funds. You can find on the account's website an investment selection page, where you might see that your employer has already preselected some investments for you. Usually, there is a mix of vehicles to choose from, including target-date funds, stock funds, bond funds, and others.[59] Your job is to pick one or more of these funds. Over time, I want you to be able to max out this account.

What does it mean to "max out?" These retirement accounts all have something called an annual contribution limit because they allow you to save on taxes.[60] The US government doesn't want us to avoid paying taxes completely, so they limit how much you can put into these accounts from your paychecks. These are annual limits from January 1 to December 31 of each year. If you are age fifty and older, you can put in an additional amount, which is called a "catch-up contribution," because the government acknowledges that you're closer to retirement and could use a little extra boost in your retirement savings. This contribution limit can increase whenever the IRS decides to increase it, usually based on inflation. Your employer may also choose to provide a match. A company match is a perk or benefit, and your employer is not required to do so.

I've seen many people make the mistake of only contributing enough to get the match and stopping there. Don't fall into this trap! The match is a perk, but the real power of these accounts is the tax savings you get because the account could either be traditional or Roth, or you can pick a combination. I want you to do your best to put as much money as you possibly can into these accounts, as early as you can, to take the most advantage of compounding interest over time.

H for Health Savings Account

People often refer to the health savings account (HSA) as the triple-tax savings account—money goes in tax-free, grows tax-free, and can be used tax-free on qualified healthcare expenses. I think HSAs are a great tax hack, but the circumstances that led to their creation feel unfair due to the high deductibles.[61] That's why, in my framework, I say that *only* if your high-deductible health plan (HDHP) is the best healthcare plan available to you should you open an HSA. (That's why the H in FHIT is silent.)

An HDHP is defined as any health plan with a minimum deductible determined by the government.[62] If you have an HDHP, you can contribute to an HSA. Most healthcare plans have an online portal to open one, and you can also open one yourself with a financial institution. The contribution limit varies, with a lower limit if you're the only person covered by the health plan and a higher limit if you have family coverage. Contributions to an HSA are traditional/ tax-deferred, meaning you can deduct them from your income taxes in the year you contribute. The money then grows tax-free inside the account. If you use the money for qualified healthcare expenses, you are not taxed on it.[63] If you are fifty-five or older, you can add $1,000 a year as a catch-up contribution. By the time you turn sixty-five, the account becomes like a traditional IRA. This means you can withdraw money without penalty (but are still subject to income taxes) for retirement.

Your HDHP might not be the best healthcare plan available. Compare the tax savings you may realize by having an HSA coupled with your HDHP against the total cost of having perhaps a lower-premium, lower-deductible healthcare plan. In many cases, it might not make sense to spring for the HDHP, especially if your other healthcare options provide more comprehensive coverage, extensive provider networks, and lower deductibles. However, if having an HDHP is the best (or only) healthcare option, maximize your contributions to an HSA. Use it for healthcare and invest any money that is left over for retirement.

I for IRA

Individual Retirement Arrangements, or IRAs, are for everyone. Anyone who has legal work status in the United States can open and contribute to an IRA in the years they earn income.[64] I place these accounts lower in importance than employer-sponsored accounts because their contribution limits are lower; you can't put as much money into these accounts as you can into 401(k)s, so that means less tax savings available. Furthermore, contributions don't automatically come from your paycheck, and the psychology of having to set aside money and move it to an IRA can sometimes be why people don't invest at all. Nevertheless, if you have the ability, I still recommend using these accounts to the best of your ability.

Anyone who reports earned income can have an IRA; this includes minors, for whom parents/guardians would set up what is known as a custodial IRA. Furthermore, if you file your taxes as "married filing jointly," as long as one spouse has earned income, both spouses can contribute to an IRA of their choosing. The technical term for the nonearning spouse's account is "spousal IRA," though you won't hear that word when you go to a financial institution or visit a brokerage's website. Just open or use a traditional or Roth IRA, like everybody else, and report according to your joint tax return.

Once you have an account open, you can transfer money and choose investments. Like your employer-sponsored accounts, the money, by default, sits in cash until you purchase an investment. Look for the Invest or Trade menu to select and purchase investments. You can contribute to an IRA for the current tax year from January 1 until April 15 of the *following* year. Every year, there are 3.5 months when you can contribute to an IRA and have it count toward two different years. For example, on February 2, 2022, I could contribute toward either the tax year 2021 or 2022. However, on May 1, 2022, my contribution counts only toward tax year 2022.

There are some income-related limits when you contribute to an IRA, which are outlined in the appendix on page 215. In general, similar to your employer-sponsored F account, I want you to do your best to max out an IRA and take advantage of its tax savings.

T for Taxable Brokerage

After all of the above, if you still have money left to invest, you may put it toward a taxable brokerage. That is incredible! The taxable brokerage is a trading account that anyone with a social security number in the US can open and trade with, regardless of whether you make income. There are no limits on how much you can contribute to a taxable brokerage, or when and how much you can withdraw from these accounts. This is because these accounts do not have any tax benefits.

Traditional versus Roth

Many people ask, "Should I contribute my money to a traditional 401(k) or Roth 401(k)? Should I contribute to a traditional IRA or Roth IRA?" Please don't let this decision be a significant hurdle to investing!

Most people put their money in traditional status if they believe they have high tax rates now and will have lower taxes in retirement. This preference is common among high-earning people who expect to withdraw in retirement much less than they earn in their highest-earning years. The opposite is usually true for those who favor Roth accounts. They typically wish to lock in the tax rate they are paying today. Or they may believe that the US government will likely increase its tax rates in the coming years and that they will inevitably have higher taxes regardless. Furthermore, having money in the Roth tax status can also be beneficial to those who wish to have the opportunity to withdraw money earlier than age 59.5.

There is no right or wrong answer. Some people might split their money between traditional and Roth tax statuses. Others might be very certain and choose one way over another. As individual circumstances vary, there is no exact formula that I can provide to guide you. If you can't decide, choose to the best of your abilities and accept the uncertainty.

Early Withdrawal

The vast majority of retirement accounts have what is known as an early-withdrawal penalty. If you withdraw from these accounts before you turn age 59.5, you owe a 10% penalty on the amount withdrawn in addition to any taxes. That doesn't bode well for people who wish to retire earlier than age 59.5, right? So how would it work? Thankfully, there are a few loopholes to help you get around this.

457(b) accounts: These accounts don't have early-withdrawal penalties. Once you leave the employer, you can access the funds without paying the penalty.

Original contributions: Your original contributions to Roth IRA accounts can be withdrawn early. These withdrawals are called "a return of your regular contributions from your Roth IRA(s)."[65]

Five-year Roth conversion rule: If you convert money from a traditional account into a Roth IRA, the converted amount becomes penalty-free five years starting from January 1 of the tax year in which you made the conversion.[66] What many early retirees do is convert just enough for one year of living expenses, once a year, until they reach age 59.5. This is called a Roth conversion ladder (page 217 in the appendix).

Rule 72(t) withdrawals: This rule allows you to take penalty-free early withdrawals from employer-sponsored retirement plans and IRA accounts if you withdraw at least five substantially equal period payments over five years. You must adhere to these withdrawals over five years or until you reach age 59.5, whichever comes later. Calculating this amount can be tricky, which is typically why most people use a good CPA who knows how to make these withdrawals.

The strategy that I devised for early retirement for myself and my husband, if the time came to that, was as follows:

- Withdraw from our taxable brokerage accounts. These accounts have no limit, and we'd also benefit from paying a lower capital gains tax rate versus an ordinary income tax rate.

- Make timely Roth IRA conversions from our 401(k) accounts. These conversions are not accessible until five years from the conversion, so, at the very least, five years of expenses should sit within our taxable brokerage and original Roth contributions.

- Take 72(t) withdrawals from our 401(k)s, only if we really need to.

Other Accounts

Here's a quick breakdown of a few more account types. (I also provide more details and examples of these in the appendix on page 216.)

Backdoor Roth: A tax loophole that high earners use to achieve the same effect as a Roth IRA.

"Mega backdoor Roth": An unofficial term for a 401(k) where the employee can contribute above the annual paycheck contribution limit and dip into the limit that is provided to the employer to use for matching the profit-sharing.[67] The employee's additional contributions go to the after-tax portion of the 401(k). The employee then needs to instruct the 401(k) administrator to do an in-service conversion to the Roth portion of the 401(k). Given its similarity to a backdoor Roth, this maneuver is called a mega backdoor Roth.

529 accounts: Accounts designed for education savings. Some states might give you a state income tax break while you put money in these accounts. The money grows tax-free, and if used on qualified educational expenses for the beneficiary, that money withdrawn is also tax free.[68] If overfunded, there are some ways to resolve this (see page 219).

ABLE accounts: These accounts are designed for disabled beneficiaries. The contribution limit is the gift-tax exclusion amount (which the IRS sets each year per donee[69]), and the money grows tax-free and can be used tax-free on qualified disability expenses.

It is normal to feel overwhelmed after reading the above information. The US tax code is so complicated. It took me several years to understand everything that I am discussing in this chapter, and I am still learning and evolving my strategy because the government can and does make changes. Take a deep breath and do things one step at a time. FHIT can help you determine the sequence in which you can focus your efforts, and then as your needs and life circumstances change, you can slowly incorporate the other accounts as they become relevant. You do not need to do it all at once. Any effort, any money that you can put aside and invest in a manner that is tax-advantaged already puts you ahead of the average American.

My Wishes for You

Personal finance and wealth-building are a lifelong journey. As confident as I sound about my situation, I often wonder what life has in store for me. How long will I live? Will there be significant warfare and turmoil that upend everything? Will I be healthy and physically strong into my seventies and eighties? There are still a lot of unknowns, and my life will never be perfect. The great thing is you are not doing this alone. Most people on this planet feel the same way about money and experience similar struggles and emotions. Use the techniques that I describe in this book to help reframe your mindset for the better, and you can and will achieve financial freedom and build wealth.

Where Are They Now?

I love happy endings, and I want to share stories of hope from the people we have met throughout the book so that you, too, can have hope for your future.

Wendy, the photographer with student loans, has manifested a series of incredible changes. She has since gotten engaged to a man who puts her and her needs first. Her financial situation has also improved, and she was able to pay off $30,000 of her loans and negotiate many of her monthly bills. She gave up an expensive cable subscription, moved toward lower-cost phone plans, and learned how to save and invest. She even started a college fund for her younger child. She has branched out in her career, left a toxic work partnership, and is developing new ideas to raise her income. She holds strong to the hope that she will be debt-free one day.

Maria, the single mother with the Feast and Famine root cause, continues to focus on what is important for her daughter and her. Based on my calculations, she should be able to save comfortably for retirement and fund a significant portion of her daughter's educational expenses; and I believe that with steady promotions at work, one of which she recently achieved, she will be able to own her own home one day.

Daisy, whose anxiety led to her taking on consumer loans before and after her divorce, took an intensive class that I taught on developing an abundance mindset. Boy, was she determined to make a change! I learned that part of the drive came from being laid off around the time she joined my class. She refinanced several of her consumer loans to a lower interest rate via a personal loan; and consolidated her student loans to the Saving on a Valuable Education program, provided by the US government. After taking my class, it was as if the faucet turned on full force. She found a new job that paid 30% more and got remarried. Her husband tripled his income that year; they bought a house and are now expecting their first child together. Daisy and her husband have the same goals, talk about finances (a big change from Daisy's first marriage), and expect to get debt-free within the next two years. Daisy says, "My life has made a total 180, and I have been blessed to receive all I ever asked God for and more. I have never felt more prepared to take on more responsibilities, especially financially, and learn about myself more deeply."

Esther and her husband, who sat on a large amount of uninvested cash, became parents. They moved across the country to be closer to family to raise their child. After years of working in startups, Esther landed a dreamy corporate job for a Fortune 500 company. Since I began coaching them, they have bought a home and changed their lifestyles to focus more on eating at home and spending time with family. They now primarily invest in low-cost index funds, have reduced how much money they keep in cash, and opened a 529 account for their child. Esther and her husband discuss their finances weekly with each other and track their spending habits regularly. They also plan their financial goals every quarter and make sure their budgets are realistic for their current stage in life, which is constantly evolving as their family grows.

My Wealth Diary, the personal-finance blogger who documented her debt-free journey on social media as she paid down her student loans, has seen her investments take off. She publicly shares her progress toward retirement and is projected to reach $1 million in net worth in 2025 at the young age of thirty.

Natalie, who took on student loans during college even though her parents provided tuition, continues to work with me through private coaching. Since 2021, her income has grown from a little over $100,000 to nearly $200,000. When Natalie moved home for a while to save money so she could buy a home of her own, her parents found out that she had taken out student loans. It was a very awkward time, but eventually her dad saw how diligent Natalie had been about rectifying her mistake: She started planning for purchases and being intentional in her spending, bought a car in cash, got a higher-paying job, pared back on expenses by limiting outings and travel, and focused on "squirreling away every dime and penny because I knew it was a rare chance to save up this much." On her thirty-sixth birthday, Natalie's dad gifted her enough money to pay off the rest of her student loans. She shed a lot of tears out of gratitude. The heavy weight of her shame and guilt for using all her loan money to party in college began to fall off her shoulders. Now, her only debt is her mortgage. She hopes to build enough "freedom to spend with family, friends, and ultimately fulfilling God's plan and will for my life, whatever that might look like." She is able to make better decisions by organizing her finances and looks at her past in a different light, with understanding and grace for herself. Based on my calculations, Natalie is likely to finish saving for her retirement by her late forties.

Danielle, whose Adverse Events root cause associated with her divorced parents led to uncontrollable spending and consumer debt, continues to find community and support through her faith in God. She leads a loving life at home with her husband and children. These days, she looks for areas where she can be grateful and find joy. Within just one year of working with me, Danielle paid off another $12,000 of her $32,000 loan balance. She expects to become debt-free within the following year and has become very intentional with her money by tracking all her expenses, learning to control her emotions, and increasing her charitable giving to the church. She realizes how hard she was on herself for being in debt and is no longer afraid of money. She writes, "I push forward, and I know I can do this. I was living in fear and scarcity. I finally understand that nothing on the outside is going to change my inside. It's about love. It's about freedom. I do feel very free."

Ayana, whose root cause of Feast and Famine led to culinary school debt, has since begun to work in educational coaching. She can afford good healthcare and still cooks for friends and loved ones in her free time. In 2024, she learned that her student loans may be eligible for forgiveness due to deceptive practices by the culinary school she'd attended, which has since shut down. As she works on her loans, she still has financial goals she wants to achieve and finds herself fighting old thoughts and mindsets. But she feels more equipped to reach her goals and step into full freedom one day.

Sammie, the woman who suffered abuse from her father and an ex-boyfriend, can now catch herself when she has fear and anxious thoughts about money. She paid down $11,000 of outstanding debt and prepaid some of her federal and state taxes so that she wouldn't incur interest. She also took out $7,700 to register for continuing-education courses for her health and well-being business. Sammie found an online high-yield savings account for her emergency funds and invested $40,000 via a taxable brokerage account. It was very difficult for her to let that money go into the risky unknown, but she took a big leap of faith, and I'm proud of her for doing so. Sammie shares, "I no longer fear that my money will all go away tomorrow and I'll be left on the street. I feel thankful to have breathing space and blessed that I have an opportunity to reclaim my financial outlook."

David, whose immigrant father told him to avoid the stock market, has since enthusiastically studied my analysis of his financial situation. His wife and he now embrace investing in the stock market with the same commitment as with their real-estate investments. They have been maxing out their employer-sponsored retirement accounts and setting up investment funds for funding their children's college funds, and they have slowed down the pace at which they were making extra payments to their low-interest mortgage loans.

Over time, Mary, whose Adverse Events root cause led her to avoid risk, began to gain more confidence in investing. A few years of therapy helped her come to terms with her chronic illness, and as she got older, she also realized she wanted to be an active participant in her husband's and her journey to secure their financial future. Driven by her innate intellectual curiosity, Mary began reading and learning from every personal-finance and investing resource she could find. She realized through our work together that she did not have to trade stocks to consider herself an investor. She finally moved $71,000 of the $160,000 in savings into the stock market. Within eighteen months of coaching, Mary and Bill crossed $1 million in net worth.

As for me, I recently saw one of my friends who's known me since my mid-twenties. "You look like you're really enjoying California!" the friend noted as we sat down for a heart-to-heart catchup on a warm summer day at my favorite bagel shop (gosh, I miss those NYC bagels). I'd gained a pound of muscle or two, my hair graying has slowed, and my skin has the glassy glow of Korean pop stars. The feeling of having fewer financial worries is indescribable. It's like waking up every day with sunshine on my face and breakfast piping hot on my nightstand. I see my life and my world differently, and I feel more joy. There is peace and confidence in my own decision-making. There is more time and energy in my mind to devote to what matters the most for me.

In the year after I left my corporate role, I saw many improvements in my life. My weight training was finally yielding results, and I recovered more quickly from a second bout of postpartum depression than I had the first time. In one single year, my household net worth grew more than what my husband and I ever made together in income. Over time, I saw that the stress and tension I carried in my head and my shoulders fell off. I woke up excited for each day and didn't feel a strong need to shuffle my feet quickly from one place to another. I even smiled more at strangers as I walked past them—not something that New Yorker Shang would do! I found myself driving around Orange County, California, with KUSC classical music in the background, the phrase "I'm joyful right now" being my top thought.

I often get asked what my next financial goal is. Truth be told, I don't really have one. My wealth has been built to a comfortable level, and now my purpose has become greater. My life today is primarily consumed with scheduling fun things for my sons to do and ensuring that they don't fight too much over one noisy airplane toy. My life has become exactly what my husband and I set out to achieve—financially free enough that we can live on one income and be involved and loving parents to our children.

Thanks to my pursuit of financial independence. I get to live a life is that I love, and I hope to positively change people's lives each day I am alive. My wish is that you will be inspired by this book to do something radically different and positive with your money story. I hope that you do it scared, but do it anyway.

NOTES

1 Bill Bengen, a retired financial advisor, first articulated this rule in 1994 as the withdrawal rate at which investors should be able to retire in any economic scenario. This concept was later popularized by a study conducted by professors at Trinity University. The 4% Rule has since been widely cited in financial media.

2 Back then, Craigslist was the most popular online marketplace to find items for sale.

3 In Wendy's case, we discovered through calling her original lender that her loans had been paid off. However, this "debt-relief" program was still charging her a monthly fee to help her manage these loans that were already paid these already-paid-off loans.

4 Robert K. Naumann et al., "The Reptilian Brain," *Current Biology* 25, no. 8 (April 20, 2015): R317–21, https://doi.org/10.1016/j.cub.2015.02.049.

5 Olivia Guy-Evans, "Fight, Flight, Freeze, or Fawn. How we respond to threats," *SimplyPsychology*, November 9, 2023, https://www.simplypsychology.org/fight-flight-freeze-fawn.html.

6 Fight is facing the event aggressively; flight is running away; freeze is being unable to move or act against the threat; and fawn is trying to please the aggressor to avoid conflict.

7 "Live U.S. Dashboard: Guarantee States," NGPF, Accessed July 23, 2024, https://www.ngpf.org/live-us-dashboard/.

8 Heather McDonold and Monique Bosco, "T. Rowe Price: Parents Putting on a Financial Facade Are More Reluctant to Discuss Money with Their Kids," T. Rowe Price, December 17, 2020, https://www.troweprice.com/content/dam/trowecorp/Press%20Release%20-%20PKM%20Financial%20Facade%20FINAL.pdf.

9 Naijie Guan et al., "Financial Stress and Depression in Adults: A Systematic Review" *PLoS ONE* 17, no. 2, February 22, 2022, https://doi.org/10.1371/journal.pone.0264041.

10 Yan Leykin, Carolyn Sewell Roberts, and Robert J. DeRubeis, "Decision-Making and Depressive Symptomatology," *Cognitive Therapy and Research* 35, no. 4 (May 4, 2010): 333–41, https://www.ncbi.nlm.nih.gov/pmc/articles/PMC3132433/.

11 This book primarily discusses the impacts of depression and anxiety on decision-making. There are additional classes of mental-health issues, including schizophrenic disorders, eating disorders, obsessive-compulsive disorders, feeding and eating disorders, etc., that are outside the scope of this book.

12 Vincent J. Felitti et al., "Relationship of Childhood Abuse and Household Dysfunction to Many of the Leading Causes of Death in Adults," *American Journal of Preventive Medicine* 14, no. 4 (May 1998): 245–58, https://doi.org/10.1016/S0749-3797(98)00017-8.

13 Henry H. Yin, Barbara J. Knowlton, and Bernard W. Balleine, "Inactivation of Dorsolateral Striatum Enhances Sensitivity to Changes in the Action-Outcome Contingency in Instrumental Conditioning," *Behavioral Brain Research* 166, no. 2 (January 30, 2006): 189–

96, https://pubmed.ncbi.nlm.nih.gov/16153716/.

14 This is often known as HELOC, or home equity line of credit, discussed in Chapter Five. The reason why it is so easy to borrow against the home is that it requires little qualification to do as long as you are not over the spending limit set by your lender.

15 "Financial Abuse Fact Sheet," NNEDV, July 2019, https://www.nnedv.org/wp-content/uploads/2019/07/Library_EJ_Financial_Abuse_Fact_Sheet.pdf.

16 Kimberly Holland, "Understanding the Causes of Child Abuse," Healthline, December 3, 2018, https://www.healthline.com/health/causes-of-child-abuse.

17 E. A. Gjelten, "How Much Will My Divorce Cost?" Nolo, June 5, 2024, https://www.nolo.com/legal-encyclopedia/ctp/cost-of-divorce.html.

18 Timothy Grall, "Custodial Mothers and Fathers and Their Child Support: 2017," U.S. Census Bureau, May 2020, https://www.census.gov/content/dam/Census/library/publications/2020/demo/p60-269.pdf.

19 "Economic Well-Being of US Households (SHED)," Board of Governors of the Federal Reserve System, February 2, 2023, https://www.federalreserve.gov/publications/2022-economic-well-being-of-us-households-in-2021-student-loans.htm.

20 Nneoma Uche, "Cost of a Master's Degree: What to Know Before You Enroll," *Forbes*, August 17, 2023, https://www.forbes.com/advisor/education/student-resources/how-much-is-a-masters-degree/.

21 Kency Nittler, "How Do School Districts Compensate Teachers for Advanced Degrees?" National Council on Teacher Quality, July 26, 2018, https://www.nctq.org/blog/How-do-school-districts-compensate-teachers-for-advanced-degrees.

22 "Cost of Attendance," Harvard Medical School, https://meded.hms.harvard.edu/md-cost-attendance.

23 Acquired, "NVIDIA CEO Jensen Huang," YouTube Video, 1:30:01, October 15, 2023, https://www.youtube.com/watch?v=y6NfxiemvHg.

24 Revolving credit is a credit line that remains available even as you pay the balance. Borrowers can access credit up to a certain amount and then have ongoing access to that amount of credit. They can repay the balance in full or make regular payments.

25 When a loan is amortized and being paid off on time, each payment results in some money going toward interest and some money toward the original balance, so the total balance reduces over time. This process of spreading a loan out over time is called amortization. The interest is spread out over the lifetime of the loan, so the borrower has the same monthly payments.

26 "Enterval Analytics, LLC, Private Student Loan Report," Enterval Analytics, June 27,

2023, https://www.enterval.com/media/files/enterval/psl/enterval-private-student-loan-report-2023-q1.pdf?v=20230627T195956.

27 Government watch groups have called out student-loan servicers for multiple service errors, including delayed billing statements, long customer service wait times, and incorrect processing. Visit https://www.consumerfinance.gov/consumer-tools/student-loans/ to submit a complaint.

28 You can have a down payment that is less than 20% of the home's value. The Federal Housing Administration (FHA) loan program facilitates low down-payment loans. Without an FHA loan, a mortgage lender is likely to charge a private mortgage insurance fee until the homeowner's total equity in the home has reached 20%.

29 If a mortgage loan has a variable rate, a borrower has a fixed rate for a period of time that can last from 25% to 50% of the loan term. Then the rate would "float" based on the prevailing mortgage rates. A balloon mortgage loan has fixed monthly payments, then the principal is due at the very end. A reverse mortgage is available to retirees ages sixty-two and older, who need to use the equity in their homes to generate retirement income. The borrower receives the home equity as a lump sum, and the loan balance (principal and interest) is due when the borrower dies, moves out permanently, or sells the home.

30 Not all car loans allow you to save money if you pay it off early. Some are calculated as precomputed interest car loans—the interest you owe is applied equally into each monthly payment. In such a case, if you pay a car loan early, you may not save on interest, as you'll be paying off all the precomputed interest.

31 For example, let's say your effective tax rate is 20%. If you contribute $10,000 to your 401(k), then 20% of that is $10,000 x 20% = $2,000, which is how much you save on income taxes. If you borrow $10,000 from your 401(k) interest-free and pay for this loan with after-tax money, then you need to make $10,000 ÷ (1 − 20%) = $12,500 to have $10,000 available for the loan.

32 This means that the medical facility or provider does not receive full payment for services. Loss of full payment is a risk that all businesses anticipate.

33 "Census Bureau Releases New Educational Attainment Data," US Census Bureau, February 16, 2023, https://www.census.gov/newsroom/press-releases/2023/educational-attainment-data.html.

34 "Fast Facts," National Center for Education Statistics, https://nces.ed.gov/fastfacts/display.asp?id=900. While most student-loan data don't track loans according to immigration status, Black, Latine, and Pacific Islander students are more likely to take on student loans as compared to white students.

35 My Wealth Diary has asked that her real name not to be shared.

36 We will be negotiating debts that are in collections. You'd know from your credit report or from the original creditor. Knowing the exact interest rates, minimum monthly payments, and due dates is not as important because negotiating debt typically leads to a one-time payment.

37 For example, suppose you had a debt with a 25% interest rate. In that case, an extra dollar paid toward this debt saves you $0.25 of interest each year for the remainder of the debt. On a debt with 5% interest rate, an extra dollar saves you just $0.05 of interest each year for the remainder of the debt.

38 Unless, of course, you acquire new debt.

39 In the early 2000s, interest rates were set quite low by the Federal Reserve due to the 2001 recession. As a result, students at that time received very low interest rates, some as low as 4%! I had a classmate who graduated and began paying down their student loans. However, the stock market was doing quite well in 2005, all the way up before the 2008 recession. This classmate realized they could either ensure that they save 4% on their loan balance or take the extra money they had and invest it to get a 10% return on the market. That meant that they netted 6% more for that extra dollar. So, it didn't make sense for this classmate to pay down their student loans before investing. This was the same phenomenon that My Wealth Diary referred to earlier. She had reasonably low interest rates on her student-loans, but could have benefited from investing and getting some higher returns at the same time.

40 Reed Hastings, "Freedom & Responsibility Culture (Version 1)," SlideShare, June 30, 2011, https://www.slideshare.net/slideshow/culture-2009/8469957.

41 Bing Chen, "Bing Chen American Advertising Federation Hall of Achievement Award," YouTube Video, 4:56, December 13, 2022, https://www.youtube.com/watch?v=ISwpwiFTovg; AHN, "Bing Chen | Uplifted Conference Las Vegas 2024 | AHN," YouTube Video, 22:34, June 11, 2024, https://www.youtube.com/watch?v=30m_QFAEVe4.

42 U.S. Bureau of Labor Statistics, https://data.bls.gov/pdq/SurveyOutputServlet.

43 "S&P 500 Index," MarketWatch, June 24, 2024, https://www.marketwatch.com/investing/index/spx/download-data?startDate=1/1/1990&endDate=06/24/2024.

44 Statista Research Department, "Inflation Rate and Federal Reserve Interest Rate Monthly in the United States," Statista, U.S. Bureau of Labor Statistics, St. Louis FRED, March 1, 2024, https://www.statista.com/statistics/1312060/us-inflation-rate-federal-reserve-interest-rate-monthly/.

45 "Dow Jones - DJIA - 100 Year Historical Chart," Macrotrends, June 25, 2024, https://www.macrotrends.net/1319/dow-jones-100-year-historical-chart.

46 Anu Madgavkar et al., "Human Capital at Work: The Value of Experience," McKinsey

& Company, June 2, 2002, https://www.mckinsey.com/capabilities/people-and-organizational-performance/our-insights/human-capital-at-work-the-value-of-experience.

47   And if someone has an edge, such as in the case of insider trading (when employees of a company use their proprietary knowledge of a company's inner dealings to buy or sell that company's stocks), there are laws against that. The federal government has regulations against insider trading that eventually catch up with the people who practice it.

48   "SPIVA," S&P Global, accessed July 30, 2024, https://www.spglobal.com/spdji/en/research-insights/spiva/.

49   Mitch Tuchman, "Day Trading Stocks Is a Guaranteed Slaughter. So Why Do It?" Marketwatch, July 6, 2020, https://www.marketwatch.com/story/day-trading-stocks-is-a-guaranteed-slaughter-so-why-do-it-2020-06-30.

50   Brad M. Barber and Terrance Odean, "Boys Will Be Boys: Gender, Overconfidence, and Common Stock Investment," *The Quarterly Journal of Economics* 116, no. 1 (February 2001): 261–92, https://doi.org/10.1162/003355301556400; "Make Way for Women Investors: Record Numbers, Higher Returns - Fidelity Study Finds 50% Increase in Women Investing Outside of Retirement, New 10-Year Analysis Reveals Women Out-Performing Men," Fidelity Newsroom, October 8, 2021, https://newsroom.fidelity.com/pressreleases/make-way-for-women-investors--record-numbers--higher-returns---fidelity-study-finds-50--increase-in-/s/eaa059ce-0a6a-41e2-ae73-838b8ff8505a.

51   A company would typically try to meet its debt obligations during bankruptcy, whereas shareholders often get nothing.

52   Jessica Dickler, "Share of Six-Figure Earners Living Paycheck to Paycheck Jumps, Report Finds. Advisor Offers Ways to Break the Cycle," CNBC, May 24, 2023, https://www.cnbc.com/2023/05/24/share-of-high-earners-living-paycheck-to-paycheck-jumps-year-over-year.html.

53   Elizabeth Renter, "Most Americans Save, but Many Can't Cover a $1,000 Emergency," NerdWallet, May 9, 2023, https://www.nerdwallet.com/article/banking/data-2023-savings-report.

54   Maartje Boer et al., "Adolescents' Intense and Problematic Social Media Use and Their Well-Being in 29 Countries," *Journal of Adolescent Health* 66, no. 6 (June 2020): S89-99, https://doi.org/10.1016/j.jadohealth.2020.02.014.

55   Christine Mikstas, "Difference Between Frozen Fruit and Fresh Fruit," WebMD, August 9, 2024, https://www.webmd.com/diet/difference-between-frozen-fruit-and-fresh-fruit

56   Frank Olito, "What the Average Person Spends on Dining Out in Every State," *Business*

Insider, August 12, 2019, https://www.businessinsider.com/what-people-spend-on-dining-out-2019-8.

57 "What is Hoarding Disorder?" Association for Behavioral Cognitive Therapies, https://www.abct.org/fact-sheets/hoarding/.

58 That is because your net worth is calculated as assets minus liabilities. Paying down debt lowers your liabilities and increases your net worth; investing increases your assets and net worth. Both lead to the same effect.

59 Many people get stuck on how to pick between these funds. As this book is not meant to provide investing advice, I strongly recommend that you do research through reading other resources on investing to create an allocation that works best for your personal situation.

60 For the tax year 2025, the employee contribution limit was $23,500, with an additional $7,500 for employees aged fifty and up.

61 "2022 Year-End Devenir HSA Research Report," Devenir, March 30, 2023, https://www.devenir.com/research/2022-year-end-devenir-hsa-research-report/.   HSAs became mainstream with the advent of the Affordable Care Act in 2010, which expanded healthcare coverage in the US to include everyone. At the same time, the legislation provided for a "Cadillac tax," which would have applied to employers who paid a lot toward employees' healthcare insurance premiums. The Cadillac tax later got repealed, but unintended damage was done, and employers keen to avoid such a tax began shifting more of the healthcare premium burden onto their employees by providing HDHPs as their primary healthcare option. On these plans, employees and their families often have to pay thousands of dollars upfront for their healthcare before any kind of insurance kicks in. HSAs were created in 2003, and by 2022, it was estimated that over ninety million Americans (around one-third of the population) used them. HSAs help employees afford their high-cost health plans (HDHPs) by offering tax breaks.

62 In 2024, this was $1,600 for an individual and $3,200 for a family, with annual out-of-pocket maximums of $8,050 and $16,100, respectively.

63 The only exception is for those who live in California and New Jersey, where contributions and capital gains are still taxed at the state level but not at the federal level.

64 The income here is defined as money you make from a job, either working for someone else or working for yourself. It doesn't include interest, dividend, and capital-gains income made from investments.

65 Let's say that over ten years, you contributed $7,000 consistently each year to a Roth IRA. After ten years, let's say that $70,000 grew to $100,000. You can now withdraw $70,000 from that account without incurring early withdrawal penalties because this was your original contribution.

66 For example, say you converted $50,000 from a traditional IRA to a Roth IRA on August 15, 2022. On January 1, 2027, you can withdraw $50,000 from the Roth IRA without penalty. However, let's say that in the five years, the $50,000 grew to $70,000; the $20,000 in growth would be subject to the 10% early-withdrawal penalty.

67 Using 2025 numbers, that means that an employee aged forty-nine or younger can contribute after-tax money up to $46,500 to their 401(k), net of any employer match and profit-sharing. In practice, most people with this capability in their retirement plans have additional limits that the corporation has put in place. You will need to check with HR on what the policies are for your particular workplace. While most employers use the extra limit for employer-matching and profit-share only, some employers also allow employees to contribute from their paychecks.

68 Qualified educational expenses for 529 accounts include tuition, room and board, and supplies at most accredited universities, colleges, and many K–12 programs and vocational schools.

69 A donee is one person to whom you gift, and you can gift to multiple people. For example, if you have two children, you may gift each child the annual gift-tax exclusion amount and have these amounts not count toward gift tax. In 2024, the exclusion amount was $18,000 per donee, and this amount can increase every year.

APPENDIX

Chapter Four

Page 79: Setting up a High-yield Savings Account

A high-yield savings account (HYSA) is an online bank account that pays more interest on your deposits compared to a conventional brick-and-mortar bank account at Bank of America or JPMorgan Chase. As these bank accounts do not have physical branches and limit the number of transactions you can make with the accounts, they pass on the savings in operating costs in the form of higher interest rates. The rates can adjust, typically in step with changes in the federal funds rate set by the Federal Reserve. I like using these accounts because they keep your emergency savings out of sight, making it more difficult for you to spend the money. Several websites provide reviews of bank accounts and current interest rates, including Bankrate.com. My recommendation is that you pick one account that has the features you like the most and don't worry about getting the highest interest rate. Most HYSAs should have interest rates that are within 0.25%–0.50% of each other. Once you pick an account, don't bother too much with moving the money around, you want it out of sight, out of mind.

Chapter Five

Page 96: Debt-free Plan

The first step in the debt-free plan is to write down and organize your debts. Here's a longer explanation for how to do that step with the table that I shared.

Name	Original balance	Current balance	Interest rate	Minimum monthly payment	Loan due date (if there is one)

Name: Give your debt a name, any name. Each debt should have its own name.

Original balance: To the best of your abilities, find out how much you originally borrowed. This doesn't have to be exact.

Current balance: Find the current balance by logging in to the appropriate website and downloading your most recent statement. Try to get this accurate to the nearest dollar.

Interest rate: If your debt is a fixed-interest-rate debt, this should be straightforward. If your debt's interest rate is variable, write down what it is today, but also note when it is expected to change. For example, if you had a promotional offer for a credit card with 0% financing for six months, note the end of the six-month promotional period.

Minimum monthly payment: Note to the cent how much your minimum monthly payment is for this debt—not how much you're sending to the debt, but what the lender wants from you at minimum. Also note if your debt is not current, meaning you have skipped or fallen behind on payments, so your balance has increased from the original. If you are behind on payments, write down how much you'd need to pay to catch up to get the debt to become current again, which puts your account in good standing and improves your credit score.

Loan due date: For debts such as mortgages, student loans, and car loans, note when the entire debt is due. You do not want this to be a surprise because if you ignore the due date, you could have a very large bill one day.

Ideally, once you have done the above, reorder the table with the debt you wish to pay off first at the top, followed by the next one, and so on so forth.

Page 97: Step 2: Save an emergency fund

If you suddenly have no income, what bills are you obligated to pay? Here is a list to consider, which you can change and add to as needed. If you're not really sure how much your emergency fund should have, give it your best guess.

- Housing (rent or mortgage)
- Minimum payments on all your loans
- Utilities
- Costs of driving your car (gas, registration fees, parking, tolls)
- Basic groceries (no lobster or caviar!)
- Internet and phone access so you can interview for jobs

- Healthcare costs (if you're laid off, you might get a few months of health insurance but then will have to pay for the rest on your own, known as a COBRA plan)

- Prescription drugs and any other medicines you take regularly

- Essential hygiene products (toilet paper, personal care, kitchen cleaning supplies)

- Child expenses, including tuition, babysitting, childcare

- Pet expenses, including pet food, vet bills, medicines

Chapter Nine

Page 169: How to budget

For a more detailed look at how to budget, I have expanded on my initial diagram with the one below. The additions show what is taken away from your gross pay before you get to your take-home pay, and it also gives more guidance as to how to allocate your spending budget once money is deposited in your bank account. Follow the diagram from top to bottom so you can see how to visualize the flow of your money from the moment you earn it to the moment you spend it. It is recommended that you calculate the below on a monthly basis.

Gross pay: This is the amount of pay you receive before any taxes, benefits, and retirement contributions are removed. If you are an hourly worker, it is your hourly pay multiplied by the hours worked. If you are a salaried worker, it is your annual salary divided by the number of paychecks received.

Taxes and benefits: Taxes typically include federal, state, and local income tax and deductions for Social Security and Medicare. Benefits typically include your portion of your healthcare premium (medical, dental, and vision health insurance) and other deductions you might have selected during open enrollment, such as health savings account (HSA) or flexible spending account (FSA) contributions, or insurance premiums. As you make more money, it is important to keep an eye on how much you are paying towards taxes and consider taking advantage of employer-sponsored retirement plans to help lower your taxable income.

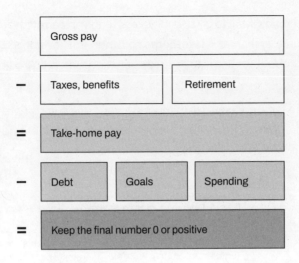

Retirement: Your retirement contributions from your paycheck are part of your overall wealth goal. For example, if your wealth goal is to contribute $500 a month toward retirement, and you already send $350 a month via your paycheck, then your remaining wealth goal is $150 a month.

Take-home pay: Your take-home pay is your net pay after taxes, benefits, and retirement contributions. It is recommended that as you learn to budget and become more aware of your overall financial situation, you move away from starting with your take-home pay and toward starting with your gross pay when designing your budget.

Debt: Paying down your debt should be prioritized in your budget. This box includes the money you pay toward your minimum debt payments as well as any additional payments you wish to pay to bring down your total balance. Refer to Chapter Five for the ideal sequence for paying down your debt.

Goals: This includes your wealth goals as well as any short- and medium-term goals that may require months or years of effort, such as saving up for a vacation, wedding, or home down payment.

Spending: After subtracting your debt and goals from your take-home pay, whatever is left is available for everyday spending on essential and nice-to-have items.

Finally, you want to be spending less than you earn. If the debt + goals + spending is greater than your take-home pay, then you have overbudgeted. The main way to correct for this is to reduce your expenses, followed by increasing your income.

For guidance around how to categorize your spending, here is a list of spending categories to consider as you create your budget and account for all your bills.

Housing	This includes rent, mortgage, escrow, utilities, taxes, condo fees, maintenance, and insurance payments.
Loans	Sum up all the minimum payments on any debts you may have (credit card, student loan, etc.) in a single month. This does not include mortgage or car payment.
Wealth	This is your savings goal. It can include money earmarked for emergency fund savings, paying extra to loans, sinking fund, or investing.
Health	Doctor's visit co-pays, and prescription drugs.
Children	Daycare, nanny, babysitters, enrichment activities, and school tuition.
Pets	Food, vet visits, prescriptions, and surgeries.
Groceries	All food and beverage purchased to be cooked at home.
Household	Cleaning supplies, appliances, maintenance.
Utilities	Phone bills, internet, water bill, etc.
Transport	Car payment, car insurance, gasoline, maintenance, parking fees, tolls and permits, public transportation.
Dining out	Takeout, coffees, and restaurant meals.
Gifting	Sinking fund recommended; don't forget about birthdays, Christmas, and anniversaries.
Travel	Sinking fund recommended.
Clothing and beauty	Apparel, accessories, shoes, hair, beauty, and personal care.
Home goods	Home décor and furniture.
Education	Continuing education, classes, and networking fees.
Entertainment	Anything you consider fun.
Other	Catch-all for everything else.

Chapter Eleven

Page 192: IRA contribution limit for tax deduction

If you decide to put your money into a traditional IRA, that means you choose to save on income taxes now. To do this, report the contribution when you file taxes (this is typically a line found in the "Adjustments to Income" section of your tax forms, and would be called "IRA deduction"), and the government will refund your taxes. However, if you make too much money, the government will no longer allow you to deduct a traditional IRA contribution. See the table below for 2024 details on this limit.

Regardless of your ability to get taxes deducted when you contribute to an IRA, you can always contribute to a traditional IRA. If you exceed the income limits, your money is in the after-tax status and not in the traditional/tax-deferred status. If you decide to put your money into a traditional IRA, you choose to save on income taxes now. To do so, you report the contribution when you file taxes, and the government will refund your taxes. However, if you make too much money, the government will no longer allow you to deduct a traditional IRA contribution.

Tax filing status			
Married filing jointly or qualifying widower	**Married filing separately** and you've lived with spouse during the year	**Single, or head of household, or married filing separately** and you did not live with spouse during the year	**Ability to contribute to a Roth IRA**
<$230,000		<$146,000	Up to the limit ($7,000 + $1,000) catch-up)
≥$230,000 <$240,000	<$10,000	≥$146,000 <$161,000	A reduced amount
≥$240,000	≥$10,000	≥$161,000	None

(Row axis label: **Your MAGI**)

MAGI: Modified adjusted gross income is defined as your adjusted gross income (AGI) with certain deductions added back, such as deductions for IRA contributions, student-loan interest, and more. You can use a MAGI calculator online to figure this out for you. As a rule of thumb, I typically take gross income and subtract traditional employer retirement contributions to arrive at a rough MAGI.

Page 194: The Backdoor Roth

There is a way for a high earner to have a Roth IRA, but it involves several extra steps and excellent tax-filing skills. The method is called a backdoor Roth IRA. You should only consider one if you exceed the income limits for contributing to a Roth IRA. The 2024 limits are above.

Unlike the traditional IRA, if you exceed an income limit, you can't contribute to a Roth IRA in that year, lest you wish to pay a penalty of 6% every year on that overcontribution until you resolve it. In general, when people are uncertain whether they'd be subject to Roth IRA limits, I suggest, when you think you're getting close, opt out altogether.

These are the steps to have a backdoor Roth IRA:

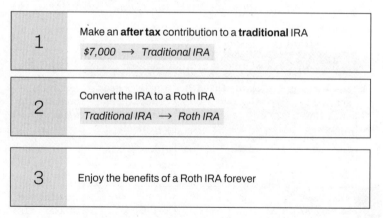

Notice that the first step is essentially putting money into a traditional IRA. (However, because you also exceed the income limits to get a tax deduction for doing so, your money is considered after tax.) Then you want to convert the funds as soon as possible to Roth tax status. Once you do so, you can invest the money going forward and not worry about more taxes!

The timing is tricky. The tax reporting for this is based on the calendar year in which you convert the money, not the year you credit your contribution. If you converted money in 2024, regardless of when you contributed that money, you'd report it on IRS form 8606 when filing your 2024 taxes in 2025. Here's a table below to give you an example.

Another thing to watch out for when trying to do the backdoor Roth is the pro rata tax. In essence, if you convert the money to a Roth IRA but still have assets separately inside a rollover IRA, traditional IRA, Savings Incentive Match Plan for Employees Individual Retirement Arrangement (SIMPLE IRA), or Simplified Employee Pension Individual Retirement Arrangement (SEP-IRA) by December 31 of the year in which you made the Roth conversion, the government essentially wants to pro-rate your Roth conversion and tax you again. Most people would like to avoid this because it is as if your contribution were taxed twice. The easiest way to prevent this is to move all the money that causes you to pay pro rata tax to a traditional 401(k) or similar account that would accept it. If you don't want to move it, then you can either convert all the money to Roth (which can mean paying a lot of taxes) or avoid the backdoor Roth IRA method altogether.

Page 193: Roth conversion ladder

In a Roth conversion ladder method for early retirement, you are converting about one year's worth of expenses into a Roth IRA account each year, with the intent of making that money available for you to withdraw penalty-free five years later. You'd do this until you reached age 59.5, after which all money from any retirement account can be withdrawn penalty-free.

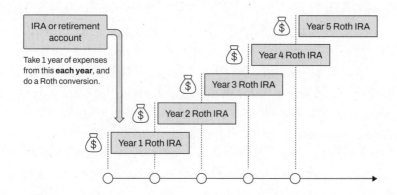

In the below image, the money in Year 1 Roth IRA becomes available to withdraw in Year 6 of this process, and so on and so forth.

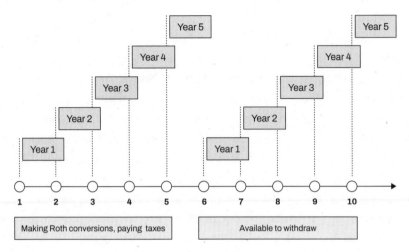

Page 189: Solo 401(k)

If you're self-employed, then as an employee, you contribute a certain amount ($23,500 for the year 2025) to a 401(k); if you're age fifty and over, you can contribute an additional catch-up amount ($7,500 for the year 2025). Then, as the employer, you can contribute up to 25% of business net earnings. For the year 2025, the $23,500 + 25% of business net earnings cannot exceed $70,000. All these limits are adjusted by the IRS regularly. There is a small catch: if you're also actively contributing to another 401(k) (perhaps you have a corporate job and you moonlight with your own company), the $23,500 limit is per person, not per account

Page 194: "Mega backdoor Roth"

A mega backdoor Roth allows you, the employee, to put money into your employer-sponsored retirement plan (typically a 401(k), but other plans have this capability as well), that exceeds the employer contribution limit. Here is an example of a mega backdoor Roth using 2024 contribution limits. This person has a $23,000 contribution limit, and their employer matches another $3,000. That means that this person has used up $26,000 of the $69,000 max for the account. This person can then contribute up to another $43,000 into the "after-tax" part of their 401(k), and then do an in-service Roth conversion right away for that $43,000. That $43,000 becomes part of the Roth 401(k) and would grow tax-free.

$70,000 account limit for <50, tax year 2025

$23,500 contributions via your paycheck	$3,000 employer match	$43,500 after tax contributions
This is the maximum employee contribution you can make.	For illustration purposes, this employer provides a $3,000 match, which is above the $23,500 employee contribution limit.	Once we subtract $23,500 + $3,000 from the account maximum of $70,000, we have $43,500. The employee can contribute this much in to the "after tax" part of your 401(k), and then you do an "in-service Roth conversion," hence the nickname "Megabackdoor Roth"

Page 194: Overfunding a 529 account

If you overfund your 529, you can change the beneficiary to another family member. If funds are ultimately not used for education, there is a withdrawal penalty of 10% on earnings and income taxes on the earnings as well. A new rule that went into effect in 2024 allows parents to roll some 529 overage amounts into a beneficiary's Roth IRA, subject to some additional fine print. The 529 must have been established for the beneficiary for at least fifteen years (this may be subject to change in the future). The lifetime maximum rollover that you can do into the beneficiary's Roth IRA is $35,000 (but may be increased in the future). The amount that can be rolled over each year is subject to the beneficiary's own Roth IRA contribution limits in that year. Contributions to the 529 in the last five years cannot be used on this Roth IRA rollover.

RESOURCES

FINANCIAL-SERVICES PROVIDERS (US only)

Fidelity
fidelity.com
Great for setting up your IRA, taxable brokerage, solo 401(k), Health Savings Account, and donor-advised fund. Fidelity has low fees and excellent customer service. Fidelity's roboadvisor, Fidelity Go, is one of the highest rated in the United States.

Schwab
schwab.com
Similar to Fidelity, Schwab also provides IRA, taxable brokerage, and solo 401(k).

Hello Nectarine
hellonectarine.com
Founded by my friend in the business, Jeremy Schneider of Personal Finance Club, Nectarine provides fiduciary, fee-only personal-finance and investing advice.

The National Association of Personal Finance Advisors
napfa.org
An association of fee-only, fiduciary financial planners.

Bankrate
bankrate.com
Up-to-date reviews on the best high-yield savings accounts, CDs, and more. Also has various retirement calculators you can use.

CNET Money
cnet.com/personal-finance
Stay up-to-date with the latest in personal-finance news.

RECOMMENDED BOOKS

The Millionaire Next Door
Thomas Stanley and William Danko
This is such an inspirational book to read about how people can save and invest their way to retirement by focusing on controlling lifestyle creep.

Broke Millennial Takes On Investing
Erin Lowry
This is a great book that dives further into the beginner concepts of investing in more detail and provides easy to understand terms and definitions.

The Simple Path to Wealth
J. L. Collins
One of the best books about investing and how simple investing can be. I recommend you read this in conjunction with *Broke Millennial Takes On Investing*.

The Bogleheads' Guide to Investing
Mel Lindauer
Can investing truly be very simple? Jack Bogle, the founder of Vanguard, believed so, and those who follow his wisdom, known as "Bogleheads," have created a book to discuss this concept.

The Power of Habit
Charles Duhigg
This book is the one that really got me thinking about how habits can influence our ability to be successful. It has several fascinating anecdotes that offer a glimpse into how businesses have used their knowledge of people's habits to gain power over consumers.

Mindset
Dr. Carol Dweck
If you want a general book about success, I highly recommend this one. Dweck has conducted groundbreaking research in the field of mindset, and this book is great reading for both students and career builders.

Give and Take
Adam Grant
Grant applies many of the teachings he provides at the University of Pennsylvania Wharton School of Business into this very accessible book, helping us network better in a world where relationships matter.

Atomic Habits
James Clear
Clear distills behavioral psychology into very easy, bite-sized strategies that you can use immediately in your own life to improve your habits, one step at a time.

Getting to Yes
Roger Fisher
Scared of negotiating? This is the book that all of my business-school classmates read as part of a negotiations course.

BLOGS AND OTHER RESOURCES
Mr. Money Mustache
mrmoneymustache.com
The original early-retirement blog that helped me feel less alone on my personal-finance journey.

Good Cheap Eats
goodcheapeats.com
The perfect blog (and accompanying cookbooks) of hundreds of delicious recipes that help you stay on budget.

Dr. Jenny Wang
asiansformentalhealth.com, Instagram: @asiansformentalhealth
Psychologist, author, and speaker who advocates for mental health with a focus on the Asian American population.

SOCIAL-MEDIA EXPERTS
Sho Dewan, Workhap
workhap.com, Instagram: @workhap
Learn how to apply, interview, and secure your next job.

Aunt Kara
Instagram: @aunt.kara
Great introductory content on how to use credit-card points and miles to travel.

Julia Menez, Geobreeze Travel
geobreezetravel.com, Instagram: @geobreezetravel
Provides pointers and strategies on how to upgrade your travel to luxury bookings.

Family Finance Mom
familyfinancemom.com, Instagram: @familyfinancemom
Well-researched content on understanding how the financial system works, from a former hedge-fund analyst.

Yo Quiero Dinero, Jannese Torres
yoquierodineropodcast.com, Instagram: @yoquierodineropodcast
A leading podcast on personal finance created by and for Latinas.

My Wealth Diary
mywealthdiary.com, Instagram: @mywealthdiary
An inspiration to follow. My Wealth Diary documents her journey to early retirement.

Frances Cook
francescook.co.nz, Instagram: @francescooknz
Author and journalist who provides personal-finance content for those living in Australia and New Zealand.

Miss Be Helpful, Yanely Espinal
mindyourmoneybook.com, Instagram: @missbehelpful
Author, financial educator, and speaker who advocates throughout the US for expanded access in high schools to personal-finance education.

Stefanie O'Connell Rodriguez
tooambitious.com, Instagram: @stefanieoconnell
Author, speaker, podcast host who is publishing a book about ambition, money, and power.

Ali and Josh Lupo, The FI Couple
theficouple.com, Instagram: @theficouple
A married couple who share their journey to financial independence through acquiring properties.

Sweet Frugal Life
Instagram: @sweetfrugallife
Tips for living on a budget, being frugal, and bargain shopping.

Allison Baggerly, Inspired Budget
inspiredbudget.com, Instagram: @inspiredbudget
Educational and very realistic personal-finance educator who teaches the basics of budgeting and does so with real people's numbers.

Jamilla Souffrant, Journey to Launch Podcast
yourjourneytofinancialfreedom.com, Instagram: @journeytolaunch
One of the best podcasts in the personal-finance space and an embodiment of the abundance mindset.

Neha Ruch, Mother Untitled
motheruntitled.com, Instagram: @motheruntitled
Author of *The Power Pause*, a guide to how to plan a career break to have children and rebound stronger than ever.